for anot[her]

Happ[y]

Love

Mikee

for anot[her]

Nā
Lei
Makamae

NĀ LEI MAKAMAE

The Treasured Lei

Marie A. McDonald
Paul R. Weissich

A Latitude 20 Book

University of Hawai'i Press
HONOLULU

08   07   06   05   04   6   5   4   3   2

Library of Congress Cataloging-in-Publication Data

McDonald, Marie A.
   Nā lei makamae : the treasured lei / Marie A. McDonald
and Paul R. Weissich.
      p.   cm.
"A Latitude 20 book."
Includes bibliographical references and index.
ISBN 0–8248–2649–3 (hardcover : alk. paper)
1. Leis—Hawaii.   2. Leis—Hawaii—Pictorial works.
I. Weissich, Paul R.   II. Title.
SB449.5.L4M34 2003
745.92'3—dc21   2003007173

Designed by Momi Cazimero

Printed by Butler and Tanner, Ltd.

Nā Lei Makamae *is dedicated to the late Frances M. Damon Holt in recognition of her many years of generous support of programs and projects focused on the conservation of the Hawaiian environment and the preservation of traditional Hawaiian culture. Of special impact was her support of the education of* keiki *whose lives were changed by an early introduction to the rich heritage of* Hawai'i Nei.

CONTENTS

FOREWORD

NĀ LEI MAKAMAE, the cherished *lei. Nā lei makamae,* the *lei* that last forever.

As youngsters growing up on Oʻahu my friends and family made and gave *lei* for many and various occasions: *ʻohana* visiting from the country or arriving from another island, or the celebration of a birthday, graduation, or wedding. *Lei* were also made when someone passed away—*ua hala ʻoia.* And as *lei* were made and given for many different reasons, they were also made and given simply for the sake of giving. There did not have to be a reason beyond the act itself. These customs and practices were merely in accord with the way we had been raised and taught. They were part and parcel of our everyday life, as they had been for countless generations past.

Our yard in Mōʻiliʻili *(ka moʻo ʻāina ʻiliʻili)* supported a variety of plants, some for eating and some for fruit and flowers. For making *lei,* we used what was available—whatever was in bloom or appropriate to the occasion and the person. This is the way things were done in our household. My elders— *tūtū kāne* and *tūtū wahine* and my aunties—showed and taught me these things, as they in turn had been taught. This is the way things were done.

Today, the making and giving of *lei* is taken for granted by nearly all who live in *Hawaiʻi nei.* It is one of many native Hawaiian practices that has survived into the modern era. Many young Hawaiians see only the outward appearance of things and understand very little or nothing about the deeper aspects of this one small part of their culture. What is detailed in this book are very old and very traditional aspects of Hawaiian culture. Each *lei,* each explanation, each word leads us to deeper understandings not only of *nā lei makamae* but also of who we are as native Hawaiians. What is revealed will leave readers with thoughts to ponder on their own.

Marie McDonald has gathered her ideas the same way as she gathers the flowers that grow around her home in Waimea. She has taken her thoughts and woven a *lei* for all of us, a *lei* of tradition and wisdom. To those who wear this *lei,* it is not to be gathered unto oneself. Rather, it is to be shared and passed on from generation to generation, as the knowledge of our ancestors was passed down from generation to generation—that we may teach those as we have been taught. This is the way things were done.

Me ke aloha pau ʻole
Abraham Piʻianaia

Note: In Hawaiian, the word "lei" is both singular and plural, depending on context. Lei is so used throughout this text.

ACKNOWLEDGMENTS

FOR THEIR GENEROUS assistance during the decade required to compile the photographs and text for this publication, we gratefully acknowledge many individuals. The work could not have been completed without their generous *kōkua*. We especially thank photographer Jean Coté for his invaluable contribution to this volume.

Each *lei* was photographed worn by a model at a site and island appropriate to the *lei*. The scope of the project meant that each Island required a coordinator to locate photo sites and to recruit models and *lei* plant sources; in many instances, they also provided ground transportation and even room and board. To these supportive people, without whose *kōkua* this publication would have been impossible, we express our sincere *mahalo nui loa:* on East Hawai'i and Lāna'i, Kepā Maly; on Kaua'i, Irmalee Pomroy; on Maui, Michael Adams; on Moloka'i, Sylvia Adams; and on O'ahu, Sarah Keahi.

For botanical and horticultural information, we are indebted to the late Dr. Charles E. Lamoureux of the Lyon Arboretum; Dr. Derral Herbst and Clyde Imada, Bishop Museum; Heidi L. Bornhorst, Honolulu Botanical Gardens; David Orr, Waimea Arboretum and Botanical Garden; Timothy W. Flynn, National Tropical Botanical Garden; Peter Van Dyke of the Amy Greenwell Ethnobotanical Garden; Richard Nakagawa and Rene Silva of the Maui Native Plant Society; Robert W. Hobdy, Maui Forestry and Wildlife Manager; David S. Boynton, Kōke'e Discovery Center; Solomon T. Kaopuiki of Lāna'i; "Chipper" Wichman and Jeff Yarberry of the National Tropical Botanical Garden's Limahuli Garden on Kaua'i; and Tim Lee of Volcano Art Center's "Niaulani."

We wish to thank Dr. Abraham Pi'ianaia, Professor Emeritus in Hawaiian Studies at the University of Hawai'i at Mānoa, who graciously consented to provide a foreword to *Nā Lei Makamae*. His thoughts and words epitomize the classical Hawaiian perception of the *lei* and set the spirit for this publication.

Very special thanks are due researcher Kepā Maly for his translations of old Hawaiian texts until now unavailable in English, and for his updated renderings of nineteenth-century English texts into contemporary language. His positive suggestions, assistance, and encouragement in many areas were basic in enabling us to produce *Nā Lei Makamae*. We are deeply indebted to him.

The word "model" implies professionals from the fashion industry; all the models photographed for this project, however, are Hawaiian or part-Hawaiian relatives, friends, and ordinary people encountered in travels around the Islands. To the 151 models—who posed patiently and pleasantly, sometimes under difficult restraints of heat, terrain, and time—we extend our deep *mahalo* and *aloha*. Models' names are listed under each photo. Unfortunately, for various reasons, not all the photos could be used. We give equal thanks to those models who gave their time but are not recognized by a published photo. *Mahalo nui loa* to you all.

Financial support from the following is gratefully acknowledged: Cooke Family Trust, Atherton Foundation, George and Lorrie Zimmer, and Faith Olelo Pa'a Ogawa. Aloha Airlines generously donated interisland flight coupons. The Friends of Honolulu Botanical Gardens provided fiscal and accounting services, and also the vehicle through which funds were channeled. Our most heartfelt thanks to our major financial supporter, who, in accordance with the donor's wishes, remains anonymous. Please accept our grateful *mahalo nui loa*.

A wide range of services and support were provided by the following, to whom we give deep thanks: Winona and Jim Adams, Roxanne Adams, Harry Kalanihi'i Arce, Patience Bacon, Santos Barbasa Jr., Deedee Lindsey Bertelmann, Linda Bertelmann, Jerry Botelho, Marcia and Michael Buratti, Emmaline Causey, Telford K. Cazimero, Jeff Chandler, Pat Clifford, John and Nat Colburn, Frank and Mavis Cook, Jennifer Crummer, James Duponte, Moana Eisele, Kaipo Frias, David Fuertes, Sherwood Greenwell, Calvin Hoe, Phil Hooton, Clyde T. Imada, Otto Cheyenne Joao, Waltham Johansen, Rubellite Johnson, Nalei and Puou Kunewa, Hālau Nā Lei o Kaholokū, Hālau o Kekuhi, Mikio Kato, Ada Kinnear, Brian Kiyabu, John Keolamaka'aina-nakalahuiokalani Lake, Len Lasalio, Robert Lindsey, Momi Lum, Brook and George Manu, Edith McKinzie, Nathan Napokā, John Obata, Patrick Paiva, Anna Palomino, Milton and Pamela Phillips, Pisces Pacifica, Walter and Paul and Noelani Pomroy, Eric and John Reppun, Greg and Marilyn Santos, Haven Santos, William Shontell, John Souza, Happy Tamanaha, Michael Tomich, Lydia Weiss, Wes Wong, and Nani Lim Yap.

Special thanks also to Don Dvokacki of Kāne'ohe for his many hours of volunteer computer assistance and to Timothy A. Culler of Ravensdale, Washington, formerly of Kailua, O'ahu, who volunteered his services to rectify a major computer problem.

"All gathering was respectful, a religious reality. The traditional lei maker was a respected, creative artist."

INTRODUCTION

CHARLES GAUDICHAUD-BEAUPRÉ was the first botanist to publish on the flora of Hawai'i. His brief visit to the Islands, in 1819, resulted in the publication of a remarkable list of his collections and, for our purposes, even more remarkable notes on the wide range of plants Hawaiians were using in making *lei*.[25]

While noting the daily wearing of *lei*, his observations did not go beyond the superficial, the decorative and physical beauty of the *lei*. He had no time to observe the deep cultural significance of the making and wearing of a *lei*, the significance of the *lei* in ritual, in *hula*, in Hawaiian myth and legend. These deeper meanings were not appreciated by Westerners until many years later.

It was, logically, the role of the earliest Hawaiian writers—Samuel Kamakau, John Papa I'i, and David Malo, among others—to note the relationship between certain *lei* and rituals. During the mid-nineteenth century, other writers publishing in Hawaiian-language newspapers provided even more extensive cultural information. These included N. J. Kapihenui, John Kihe, Stephen Desha, and Julia Keonaona.

We are also indebted to late-nineteenth-century Westerners, such as Abraham Fornander and Nathaniel Emerson, for recording and translating a wealth of oral history, much of it shedding additional light on the *lei*-culture relationship. These writers and others conserved the great traditions of the classical period of Hawai'i.

The purpose of this book, which deals with *lei* fashioned solely from flowers and plant parts, is to present and conserve the results of a lifetime of dedicated research, the culmination of a long-term, passionate effort in the areas of collecting and recording information and in propagating that knowledge through education. We wish to demonstrate that the *lei* is a classical art form deeply associated with all aspects of traditional Hawaiian life. The contents of this book will be a revelation to many, a source of inspiration for others, and, for Hawaiians, a source of pride. We also wish to enhance public awareness of the critical need for conserving our native flora, the source of *nā lei makamae*.

THE CONCEPT of the traditional Hawaiian *lei* is difficult for non-Hawaiians, and also many modern westernized Hawaiians, to understand.[29] Hawaiian men and women of old lived as an integral part of their environment. They viewed natural phenomena as bodily forms assumed by nature gods or nature spirits, which were part of their daily experience, formed the tightly woven fabric of their reality, and determined their sense of religious obligation and their standards of good and evil, of cause and effect.

From Hawaiians' sense of oneness with their world evolved the concept of *kino lau*, whereby a leaf, a flower, a stream did not *represent* a deity but *was* at any moment one of the physical manifestations of that deity. Animate and inanimate objects alike could be *kino lau*, commanding instant and unquestioned reverence and respect.

No doubt rooted in the most ancient times in Polynesia, the *lei* became part of the explosion of cultural creativity throughout the Hawaiian Islands following the cessation of contact with East and Central Polynesia, possibly around A.D. 1275.[44] Before that time, one archeologist notes that by A.D. 1100, approximately five hundred years after the initial colonization of the Hawaiian archipelago, descendants of the original settlers had developed a material culture significantly distinct from that of the ancestral East and Central Polynesians: a uniquely Hawaiian culture had come into existence.[44] After the early developmental period, the population of the Islands doubled and redoubled. With population growth, the settling of all the Hawaiian Islands, and the passage of time, Hawaiian culture burgeoned and developed into the singular forms noted by early Western explorers some five hundred years later.

Great advances were made in technique and in the production of *kapa* (bark cloth) in texture, patterning, and coloring. Featherwork developed to a high degree, and work in wood and stone became more sophisticated. The *hula* and attendant chants evolved into a unique art form. The *lei* became an extraordinarily beautiful expression of the culture itself, visible and tangible evidence of both mystical and emotional content. These advances in every aspect of material culture had, by now, grown into art forms far superior to those of their cultural roots.

A *lei* represents, in a sense, the mores of Hawaiian society and is an essential part of daily family and community life. Traditionally, a *lei* might be fashioned as a direct, specific, reverent offering to one or more of the numerous gods and goddesses who controlled the daily lives of the people and determined the fortunes of the community. A *lei* to be used in the *hula* would be made following strict rules of selection. Or a *lei* might be fashioned as a gift to honor the recipient, as a token of love, or simply as an ornament to express joy over a family occasion or something as everyday as a walk through the forest.

The *lei* maker gathering flowers and other materials, especially those that are *kino lau*, was required to recite special prayers to the appropriate deity or, for lesser materials, a simple prayer requesting permission to enter the forest to collect. Only enough material for fashioning the *lei* was gathered, thus conserving the resource and avoiding offense to the deity. All gathering was respectful, a religious reality. The traditional *lei* maker was a respected, creative artist.

Because of the protocol of gathering flowers and foliage, especially those that are *kino lau*, the voicing of a proper gathering chant is the first step in the art of *lei* making. Several gathering chants appear in the text where appropriate to the *lei* or to its cultural significance.

Our presentation of *nā lei makamae* is alphabetical by Hawaiian plant name. Many Hawaiian plants have more than one common name. We are indebted to Michael P. McKenney for his generous permission to use his unpublished list of Hawaiian plant-name synonyms, the product of more than two decades of research. McKenney's sources are the *Flora of the Hawaiian Islands,* by William Hillebrand; Joseph Rock's *Indigenous Trees of the Hawaiian Islands* and his "List of Hawaiian Plant Names"; both the 1971 and 1986 editions of the *Hawaiian Dictionary* by Mary Kawena Pukui and Samuel H. Elbert; *Flora Hawaiiensis,* by Otto Degener; and *In Gardens of Hawaii,* by Marie Neal. Priority for the selected Hawaiian name was determined by the *Hawaiian Dictionary* with but one or two deviations (e.g., *manono*). The plant names, arranged alphabetically and with synonyms, are listed in Appendix A and also in the index.

Resource material is referenced in the text by superscript numbers, which relate to authors' names listed alphabetically in the references section. For example, superscript 5 leads the reader to Martha W. Beckwith's *Hawaiian Mythology.* Selected references include page numbers for specific subjects within that reference. (E.g., reference number 5 includes "p. 187, legend of Kaohelo [*lei ʻōhelo*]." On p. 187 in Martha Beckwith's *Hawaiian Mythology,* under the heading "Legend of Kaohelo," readers will find mention of *lei ʻōhelo.*)

The majority of the *lei* described here are directly linked to published works. There are, however, eighteen for which specific written sources have not been located but for which local

cultural tradition among experienced *lei* makers makes a strong case. These *lei* display one or more of the characteristics that written sources attribute to *nā lei makamae,* particularly those with yellow or red flowers, or fruit indicative of divine and chiefly rank,[5] or purple flowers or fruit,[64] or with fragrance and thereby associated with deity.[5] One source states that Hawaiians "use all the fragrant plants, all flowers and even colored fruits" for *lei* making.[25] Several *lei* are referred to only minimally in written source material. Because of their long-standing place in the oral tradition, however, we have elected to include the following *lei: 'ākia, alahe'e, 'iliahi* and *'iliahialo'e, koai'a,* the four *lei pāpahi, manono, naupaka kahakai, nehe, 'ōhā, 'ōlapa, 'ōlulu, po'olā nui, pua 'ala,* and *uhiuhi.* In the text, these are indicated by (✐).

Most of the *lei* texts are enhanced by poems created by Pualani Kanaka'ole Kanahele, master *kumu hula,* linguist, and ethnologist (indicated after a poem as "P. K. K."). Although contemporary, they reflect traditional chant form and word usage, and convey *kaona* (hidden meanings, references below the surface), setting an appropriate mood for understanding the significance of each *lei.* For some chant translations, Kepā Maly (indicated after a poem as "K. M.") made slight modifications and added diacriticals.

Marie McDonald has created four contemporary *lei* traditional in materials and form, paralleling Pualani Kanaka'ole Kanahele's poetry composed in traditional form and language. These contemporary offerings in poetry and *lei* illustrate that the creativity of experienced, traditional artists still thrives in Hawai'i. More than a bridge from the past to the present, this is a demonstration of the continuum of cultural practices and excellence.

The four contemporary *lei* are *lei Hualālai mauka, lei Kohala mauka, lei Kuku'ena,* and *lei Poli'ahu.* All are fashioned from traditional *lei* flowers, flower buds, fruit, and/or *liko* (leaf

buds), using one or more of the methods of *lei* making that have been passed down from generation to generation: *lei haku* (arranged in a braid); *lei hili* (braided, plaited); *lei humupapa* (sewn to a backing); *lei kīpu'u* (knotted); *lei kui* (pierced and strung); and *lei wili* (a winding technique).

For scientific nomenclature, habitat description, elevation range, and plant size, we have followed the *Manual of the Flowering Plants of Hawai'i.*[68] For ferns, we have followed the nomenclature as published in *Ferns of Hawai'i.*[67]

Although many of the techniques used for making *lei* are documented in historical resource material, the structure of a *lei* may also be determined by the *lei* maker. It is part of the creativity involved in this particular art form. Experienced *lei* makers know from the size, shape, and texture of the *lei* material which technique or techniques may best be employed. This knowledge has been passed down from one generation to the next, in much the same way as have the movements, sounds, and tempos of the *hula,* or the vocal character of a chant. These are ephemeral arts: once a *hula* has been performed, its movements and sounds are gone. So it is with the short-lived beauty of the *lei.*

All *lei* discussed and pictured here were made by Marie McDonald, with the exception of five, which were generously provided as follows: *lei 'ilima* by Honey Kailio, *lei kāmakahala* by David S. Boynton, *lei mokihana* by Phyllis K. Correia, a reconstruction of *lei palaoa wiliwili* by Patrick Horimoto, and *lei po'olā nui* by Irmalee Pomroy.

The photographer, Jean Coté, is an award-winning artist of many years' experience in both the private and public sectors. He attracted early attention with his aerial photography during the Vietnam conflict. All photos are by Coté with the following exceptions: *lei 'ōlulu, lei pua 'ala, lei puapualenalena (hīnano), lei mānewanewa* and habitat, *lei 'ilima* and *lei-o-Hi'iaka (alani)* and habitat by

Roen McDonald Hufford. The habitat photo of *'ōlulu* was taken by Kenneth R. Wood, National Tropical Botanical Garden, and *pua 'ala* by Steven P. Perlman, also of the National Tropical Botanical Garden. We thank the Garden for permission to use both photos. *Kāmakahala* and *a'e* site and *lei* photos are by David S. Boynton. *Lei kūpaoa* and *lei 'ōhi'a 'ai* photos were taken by Kelvin Nakano. The photo of the pale pink fruit of *'ōhi'a 'ai* was provided by James R. Judd III.

Each site photo was taken at a location appropriate to each *lei*. Many Hawaiian plants are found on only one island or are unique to a particular site. For example, *lei po'olā nui* was photographed on Kaua'i, where it occurs, while the *lei* of red *'ōhi'a lehua* was photographed at Kīlauea Volcano on Hawai'i, as referenced in the Pele myth.

Today, much of the native Hawaiian flora is threatened, and many species are endangered. We strongly urge anyone who normally gathers *lei* material from the wild to realize that many of the plants depicted in *Nā Lei Makamae* can be grown under cultivation, thus removing pressure from wild populations. Toward this end, Appendix B provides a complete list of the *lei* plants, simple directions for their propagation, and sources of propagating material other than from the wild.

Much work remains to uncover additional information about *nā lei makamae*. Many yet untranslated Hawaiian texts and chants are in the public archives, the Bishop Museum, and private collections. We hope this publication will inspire additional research toward enhancing the understanding and appreciation of the creativity and rich cultural heritage of the Hawaiian people as revealed by *nā lei makamae*.

Paul R. Weissich
Director Emeritus
Honolulu Botanical Gardens

"A lei represents, in a sense, the mores of Hawaiian society and is an essential part of daily family and community life."

O ka lei he hiʻiaka mea hoʻokahi
He kāhiko nou mai kēia ʻāina aloha mai

The *lei* is a reflection of oneness
From this loving land,
    an adornment for you

—*Pualani Kanakaʻole Kanahele*

ʻAʻaliʻi
Dodonaea viscosa

Known for its resiliency and tenacity under difficult conditions, *ʻaʻaliʻi* grows in exposed, windy, dry areas, as well as in wet places, from sea level to elevations of 8,000 feet on all the Islands except Kahoʻolawe. In dry, windy sites it is usually seen as a shrub growing to 6 feet tall, while in wet areas it may attain small tree size, reaching to 24 feet. Its papery seed capsules, varying in color from almost white through pink to dark reddish purple, are highly favored for making *lei.*[1] In Kaʻū, this plant is called *ʻaʻaliʻi-kū-makani,* which translates "rooted like a lord standing erect in the wind."[30] Laka is the goddess of the deep-rooted *ʻaʻaliʻi.*[18] (See also reference 54.)

Kamalani Donato and Kawaiola Rapa, Kaʻa, Lānaʻi

Previous page: **Lei haku ʻaʻaliʻi**

ʻAʻaliʻi

Dodonaea viscosa

He ʻula helo, he ʻula koko, he ʻula wena
He hoa paʻa mau no ka makani Kīpuʻupuʻu
ʻĀʻo ia ʻo ʻaʻaliʻi o uka kū makani

I am pink, blood red, rosy
A constant companion for Kīpuʻupuʻu
This is indeed the *ʻaʻaliʻi* of the upland
Braving the wind
—P. K. K.

Kehaulani Ward,
ʻŌuli, Hawaiʻi

A'e

Sapindus saponaria

A large tree native to Hawai'i and many other tropical areas, *a'e* is found in the Hawaiian archipelago only on the island of Hawai'i. It inhabits semi-dry forests at Kīlauea and on Mauna Loa and Hualālai, at elevations between 2,700 and 4,000 feet.

The jet black, spherical seeds from *a'e* are popular for stringing into a long-lasting *lei*.[54] The pulp surrounding the seeds contains saponin, which was used in days gone by to produce a useful lather for shampooing hair and washing clothes.

A closely related endemic tree, *lonomea* (not pictured), is found only on Kaua'i and O'ahu. Its seeds, somewhat similar to those of *a'e*, are equally sought by the *lei* maker.

Kia Kailimoku, Kāne'ohe, O'ahu

5

A'e
Zanthoxylum dipetalum

Aplant species different from the *a'e* described above but also known as *"a'e"* grows from dry forests to the edges of wet forests on Kaua'i, O'ahu, Moloka'i, and Hawai'i. This *a'e* is a handsome, endemic tree, sometimes reaching heights of 45 feet. The foliage is dark green, aromatic, and glossy. Its seed pods and round, jet black seeds are used to fashion *lei*.[54] Several species exist. One from Moloka'i, Lāna'i, Maui, and Hawai'i is reported to bear strongly lemon-scented foliage;[57] although there is no record of these leaves being used by *lei* makers, it would be within the tradition of *lei* making.

Kekai Ikena'i Brown, Kōke'e, Kaua'i

6

'Ahu'awa
Mariscus javanicus

'Ahu'awa, found in tropical Africa and Asia and throughout the Hawaiian Islands, is a swamp or bog plant growing to several feet high. The inflorescence may be used in *lei,* and the stem may be pounded to produce a sieve for straining *'awa.*

The legend of Kalelealuakā describes an exceptional young warrior in the service of King Kākuhihewa of 'Ewa during the battles for control of the island of O'ahu. Kalelealuakā had magical powers and great strength: he could fly, leap cliffs, and run on water. In preparation for the first of several battles, Kalelealuakā flew to Wai'anae, where

he arrayed himself with *lei* of *maile lau li'i.* For the second, he flew to Waialua, where he collected *'ahu'awa,* and to Ka'ena to pick *hinahina kū kahakai.* These he fashioned into a *lei* that disguised him as a middle-aged man. For the next battle, he disguised himself as an old man by making a *lei po'o* of *kō* accented by *lei hala.* The disguises enabled his successful predawn entry into the enemy camp, where he surprised and readily overcame the enemy chiefs. The forces of Kākuhihewa prevailed.[66] (See also p. 40.)

Palikiko Apiando,
lei *with* **hinahina kū kahakai,**
Hale'iwa, O'ahu

Wīwī a loloa ke kino
Me he kumu niu
Ho'olō'ihi loa nā lau mio
Me he puapua o ka manu lele
'Ā'ula ka 'āhui pua
Me he kāhili ali'i
'O ka 'ahu'awa nō ia

The body is thin and tall
Like the coconut tree
The slender leaves are extremely long
Like tail feathers of a flying bird
The flower cluster is reddish brown
Like the royal feathered staff
This is indeed *'ahu'awa*

—P. K. K.

7

'Aiakanēnē
Coprosma ernodeoides

An endemic, prostrate shrub, *'aiakanēnē* grows on Hawai'i and East Maui at elevations of 3,000 feet to over 7,000 feet. It commonly inhabits open, sunny areas, in both *'a'ā* and *pāhoehoe.* The leaves, flowers, and jet black fruit are used by the *lei* maker. (See photographs in *lei pāpahi* section, p. 64.)

'Ākia
Wikstroemia pulcherrima

Of the dozen species of *'ākia* endemic to the Hawaiian Islands, the one pictured here bears the largest and most ornamental fruit. Growing in windswept fields on the dry side of Waimea on Hawai'i at elevations between 2,000 and 3,000 feet, this *'ākia* is a dense shrub that may reach 6 feet tall. The bright orange-red fruit are plentiful in season and are used to fashion *lei.*

'Ākia has medicinal qualities, and *kūpuna* (elders) relate that stringing the fruit provided an easy way of transporting it without bruising or crushing it. The bark provides a strong fiber used to make ropes, braids, and *kapa* (bark cloth). *'Ākia* roots, bark, and leaves may be pounded to release a chemical that narcotizes fish, used as an aid in catching them in shallow saltwater pools.

Hahakuola, Iokepa, Hukakehanokalani,
and Puau'ilaumaikalani Chong,
Waiki'i, Hawai'i

Aia i uka ka 'ākia
Lehiwa ka hua pala 'alani i ka mea 'auana
'Ako 'ia, kui'ia a ho'olei'ia ka 'ākia
He lei 'ā'ī 'alani
He nani!

The *'ākia* is in the upland
The ripened orange fruit attracts the wanderer
The *'ākia* is plucked, sewn and worn
An orange neck *lei*
A beauty!
—*P. K. K.*

9

'Ākōlea

Athyrium microphyllum

Found in wet places throughout Hawai'i at elevations between 2,000 and 6,000 feet, the beautiful fern *'ākōlea* is used in making *lei*.[18] Under ideal conditions, the fronds may grow more than 3 feet long. On Kaua'i, *'ākōlea* was one of the plants placed on the *kuahu hula* (the hula altar),[4] which indicates the plant's high cultural status.

New *'ākōlea* foliage is pinkish red, the "garland of red" described in the following chant:[18]

Kahanakumu'ole Kirn, Kealakekua, Hawai'i

Kāhuli aku	Land snails
Kāhuli mai	Trilling in the distance,
Kāhuli lei 'ula	Trilling nearby,
Lei 'ākōlea	Adorned in a garland of red.
Kōlea, kōlea	Fetch some water,
Ki'i ka wai	Water of 'Ākōlea.
Wai 'ākōlea.	—K. M.

Lei 'ākōlea
Kōlea, o kōlea.

Kupaianaha ka nani, 'o 'ākōlea
Ke luli nei nā alolua, 'o Wākea lāua 'o Papa
Ā e hilo'ia ana 'o 'ākōlea i lūlō pono
No nā lani

The beauty of *'ākōlea* is extraordinary
Wākea and Papa, the duo, nod approvingly
And *'ākōlea* is woven into a *lei* befitting
The gods
—P. K. K.

ʻĀkulikuli ʻAeʻae
Lycium sandwicense

ʻĀkulikuli ʻaeʻae is a spreading, succulent shrub that grows to 3 feet high. It flourishes in windy, dry, sometimes salty, rocky places along the coasts of all Islands and bears insignificant flowers but small, bright-red fruit prized in making *lei*.[19] Once common, it is now an endangered species.

In the Pele and Hiʻiaka myth, Hiʻiaka, on returning to Kīlauea from Kauaʻi with Chief Lohiʻau, stopped at what is now Pearl Harbor and offered the following chant.[19] Note the three different plants named for making *lei*.

Kuʻu ʻaikāne i ke ʻawa lau o Puʻuloa
Mai ke kula o Peʻekāua, ke noho ʻoe,
E noho kāua e kui, e lei i ka pua o ke kaunaʻoa,
I ka pua o ke ʻākulikuli, o ka wiliwili.

My companion is at the many-harbored bay of
    Puʻuloa
You dwell upon and come from the plain of
    Peʻekāua
Let us two sit and twine a garland of *kaunaʻoa,*
With blossoms of the *ʻākulikuli* and *wiliwili.*
—K. M.

Ua ʻako ʻia ka ʻākulikuli ʻaeʻae
E ka wahine kui lei ma Maʻalaea
Ua wilia ka lei hua me he kaunaʻoa
E hoʻolei ʻia ana e ka malihini auana

The *ʻākulikuli ʻaeʻae* is plucked
By the *lei*-stringing woman at Maʻalaea
The *lei hua* is woven with *kaunaʻoa*
To be worn by the wandering stranger
—P. K. K.

Healani Kealoha with **lei kaunaʻoa**, *Paniau, Hawaiʻi*

Alahe'e

Canthium odoratum

lahe'e bears shiny foliage and abundant clusters of white, extremely fragrant flowers, and the two attract the *lei* maker. Usually seen as a shrub, *alahe'e* may grow as a small tree, attaining heights of 40 feet under optimum growing conditions. *Alahe'e* is found on all the Islands except Ni'ihau and Kaho'olawe. It tolerates a wide range of conditions, from dry, windswept coastal areas to wet forestland at elevations up to 2,500 feet.

Mapu ka hanu o alahe'e i ka pō
Hūlali nā lau i ka Māhealani
He kumu pa'a 'Ōlelo Moana
He hō'ailona pono, ola ka 'āina

The fragrant *alahe'e* perfumes the night air
The leaves glisten in the moonlight
It is a stalwart tree at 'Ōlelo Moana
A good omen, the land is healthy

—P. K. K.

Kilohana Domingo, Pu'uhonua-o-Hōnaunau, Hawai'i

Alani (Lei-o-Hi'iaka)
Melicope oahuensis

Closely related to the cherished *mokihana* of Kaua'i, this O'ahu *alani* is a shrub or small tree growing at elevations between 1,200 and 2,500 feet. The leaves when crushed emit a strong anise fragrance.[14] It is also known on Maui.

Forty-seven species of *alani* grow in the Hawaiian archipelago. Some are shrubs, others small trees. Many contain aromatic oils in the foliage and fruit. They are found in a variety of habitats, ranging from semi-dry to wet, at elevations from less than 1,000 feet to 4,000 feet. The species in the *lei* pictured is from O'ahu, found in both the Wai'anae and Ko'olau Ranges.[33]

Alani leaves and aromatic fruit are used in a *lei* called *lei-o-Hi'iaka*,[54] referring to the goddess Hi'iaka's travels through the Wai'anae Range on O'ahu during her return to Hawai'i from Kaua'i.[33] From the height of Pōhākea, on O'ahu, Hi'iaka looked down and saw that Pele had destroyed Hi'iaka's sacred *'ōhi'a* groves in Puna. With this, Pele had broken her promise to Hi'iaka, which negated Hi'iaka's former intense loyalty to the fire goddess, thereby affecting the dramatic outcome of the story.[19]

Noelani Iokepa, **lei** *with* **palai**, *Wai'anae, O'ahu*

'O Hi'ilei ka lei o Hi'iaka
Mai ke kumu alani mai
No O'ahu a Lua
Kui ka 'ano'ano alani
No ke kūpaoa i ka hale pili

The favorite is the *lei* of Hi'iaka
From the indigenous *alani*
Belonging to Lua's O'ahu
String the *alani* seeds
For the permeating bouquet in the grassy abode
—*P. K. K.*

'Awapuhi
Zingiber zerumbet

Probably native to the tropics of Southeast Asia, *'awapuhi* (shampoo ginger) was from ancient times widely spread by colonizing voyagers. It was early introduced into Hawai'i and valued for many uses, which included scenting of stored *kapa*, as a flavoring for meat, and, because of the saponification of its sap during inflorescence, as a shampoo. Today, *'awapuhi* is a common ground cover in moist, shaded lowland areas on all the main Islands except Ni'ihau and Kaho'olawe. Under optimal conditions, *'awapuhi* may grow to be 5 feet tall.

Combined with two other Polynesian introductions, *mai'a* and *kī*, *'awapuhi* is fashioned into a *lei* worn by surfers to provide protection against dangers of the sea.[30] All three plants are linked with the god Kanaloa, who is associated with the sea. On both Maui and Kaua'i, *'awapuhi* stems were added to the five traditional plants placed on the *kuahu hula*.[4]

Imaikalani Makanani, lei *with* lā'ī *and* mai'a, Kahinihini'ula, Hawai'i

Hilo nā lau 'awapuhi
Pē'ia e ka lima hana
Ho'opuīa 'ala 'o 'awapuhi
I kahi uli o ka wao kahakai
E honi i ke 'ala ma ka po'ohiwi
E walea i ke 'ala ma ka umauma

'Awapuhi leaves
Crushed by plaiting fingers
Exude the fragrances
In secret, shaded, forest places
Inhale the perfume on the shoulder
Enjoy the perfume on the breast
—*P. K. K.*

'Āwikiwiki

Canavalia galeata and *C. hawaiiensis*

At low, somewhat dry elevations, tangles of *'āwikiwiki* vine clamber over shrubs and small trees, displaying clusters of the brilliant blossoms sought by the *lei* maker.[25] The six native species, several restricted to but one island, bear flowers varying from deep purple to rose purple, magenta, and carmine to pink and, rarely, white. (See also reference 61.) The purple-flowered species shown in the photographs occur on O'ahu, and the dark carmine-flowered species is found on Lāna'i, Maui, and Hawai'i.

He aha ka hana a ka 'āwikiwiki?
Kū a'e, moe ihola, kū a'e, moe ihola
Pa'a 'ula 'ula i ke kui 'ana
I ka lei aloha

What is the *'āwikiwiki* doing?
Up, down, up, down
Redness overflows when stringing
The *lei* of love
—P. K. K.

Kapuhealani Adams, Kanahā, Maui and Hiko'ula Hanapī, Moanalua, O'ahu

15

Hala
Pandanus tectorius

Hala (screwpine), possibly native to Hawai'i, grows as a small tree up to 30 feet tall, with a wide-spreading canopy. It occurs throughout the tropical Pacific to Indonesia and northern Australia and on all the Hawaiian Islands except Kaho'olawe. It is a lowland plant, commonly growing along moist coasts and windward valleys to elevations of about 1,800 feet. Besides being valued in *lei* making, the *hala* plant is a resource for numerous other uses: cordage, brushes for decorating *kapa*, and leaves for plaiting and thatch.[41] (See also *hīnano.*)

Male and female flowers of the *hala* are borne on separate trees. The female tree bears fruit, composed of several colored segments tightly fitted together in a roughly spherical shape. Each segment contains seeds. *Lei hala* is made from the colored segments, which are harvested by the *lei* maker before the entire fruiting body matures.

The Hawaiian culture reflects a strange dichotomy of perception toward the wearing of a *lei hala*. For example, in Nathaniel B. Emerson's translation of the Pele and Hi'iaka myth, *lei hala* are mentioned several times, noting Hi'iaka's wearing *lei hala* and that *lei hala* is favored by Kapo.[19] The early botanist Charles Gaudichaud noted its popularity.[25] The fragrance as well as the color are frequently noted. Yet the word *"hala"* is translated as sin, vice, offense, fault, error, or failure, and at certain times the *lei* was not worn because it was believed to bring bad luck.[54]

At least six color variations of the fruit segments are known and are frequently used by the *lei* maker.[54]

hala.   The common yellow to red fruit sections used in *lei*.

hala ʻīkoi.   Lemon colored at base, bright orange in upper half.

hala lihilihi ʻula.   Bright yellow at base, changing to bright orange-red at the top of the fruit segment.

hala melemele.   Bright yellow fruit segments.

hala pia.   Small, canary-yellow fruit segments prized for *lei* and for medicinal purposes, especially those used for exorcising evil spirits (not shown).

hala ʻula.   Entire fruit segments red orange.

Lei hala ʻula carried great ceremonial significance. In the ritual of selecting and collecting *ʻōhiʻa* logs from which to carve images, and the dedication of those images at a new *heiau luakini* (temple for human sacrifice), the following is recorded involving the use of *lei hala ʻula*.

The *ʻalaea* priest (one whose faced was daubed with *ʻalaea*, the red earth used for coloring salt, for medicine, and as a dye) led the purification ceremony called *hiʻuwai*. Three *lei hala ʻula* were carried to the purification ceremony. One the *ʻalaea* priest placed around the neck of the king, another around the neck of the image carved from the *ʻōhiʻa* log, and the third around his own neck.[34]

Keolamakaʻāinanakalahuiokalani Lake,
hala ʻula,
Kahaluʻu, Hawaiʻi

Hala
Pandanus tectorius

Hala ka moani
Halihali'ia ke 'ala o ka hala
I ka uka o ka Puna
E aloha i ka po'e o uka i ka lua

The windblown fragrance passes
The perfume of the *hala* is being carried
To the uplands of Puna
To greet the family at the crater   —*P. K. K.*

Above: *Maile Botielho, hala 'īkoi,*
    Waimea, Hawai'i
Top left: Iona Ka'apana, hala 'ula,
    Waiākea, Hawai'i
Bottom left: Kaleonapua Weller, hala lihilihi 'ula,
    Pu'ukapu, Hawai'i
Opposite page: Tamara Whitehead, hala pia,
    Paniau, Hawai'i

19

Hala Pepe

Pleomele hawaiiensis

Sacred to Laka, goddess of *hula*, *hala pepe* is one of the plants that was placed on the *kuahu hula*.[18] (See also reference 4.) A large shrub or small tree, the species of *hala pepe* pictured here usually grows to 15 or 20 feet tall, bearing masses of pendant, greenish yellow flowers, which are gathered by the *lei* maker.[18] Once common in dry areas of Kona on the Big Island, at elevations between 1,500 and 2,400 feet, this *hala pepe* is now rare and endangered.

The gathering of poles, greenery, and other materials used in making and decorating the *kuahu hula* and its enclosure was accompanied by prayers addressed to the innumerable wood spirits from whose realm the materials were garnered. There were

'O ke kupuna o ka 'āina ka hala pepe
Ua kapu'ia e Laka nona iho
E kūlou i ke aka kupuna o Hawai'i

Hala pepe is the ancestor of the land
Made sacred by Laka for herself
Give deference to the ancestral essence of Hawai'i
—P. K. K.

many forms of prayer—formal, informal, and even spontaneously composed on the spot. They were appeals for permission to collect and were intended to thank and placate the spirits. (See *'ie'ie*, p. 26.)

Note: Flowers used in making the *lei* pictured were collected entirely from cultivated plants.

Hualālai and Pualilia Keahuloa, Pu'uwa'awa'a, Hawai'i

Hau
Hibiscus tiliaceus

otanists are undecided whether *hau* is native to the Islands or was another Polynesian introduction during the period of migration from the south. It grows along coasts and in wet valleys on all the Islands except Niʻihau and Kahoʻolawe. Early travelers recorded its use in *lei*.[25] Its plentiful bright-yellow flowers marked it for a popular *lei*. *Hau* was also the source of a strong fiber, sometimes used by the *lei* maker, and the flowers and bark were employed medicinally.

Inu ka wai pua, he lāʻau, nani lā
ʻIhi ka ʻili, he kaula, paʻa lā
Pua mele i ke kakahiaka, ʻuweke lā
Hāʻulaʻula i ke ahiahi, hala lā

Drink the flower sap, healing, splendid
Strip the bark, a rope, tough
Yellow flower in the morning, opening
Orange red in the evening, ending

—*P. K. K.*

Top left: Tommy Tokioka, Holoholokū, Kauaʻi
Bottom left: Kapiʻolani Ching, Holoholokū, Kauaʻi

21

Hinahina Kū Kahakai
Heliotropium anomalum var. *argenteum*

Hinahina kū kahakai grows in sandy beach sites and rocky coastal areas subjected to buffeting salt winds on all the Hawaiian Islands. An endemic form of *hinahina*, it is a flat, spreading ground cover only a few to several inches tall. *Hinahina* flowers are sweetly fragrant, varying in color from white to pale purple.

The plant's fragrant flowers, silvery white succulent foliage, and long life after picking render it highly attractive to the *lei* maker. (See also *'ahu'awa*, p. 7). Emerson's *Unwritten Literature of Hawaii: The Sacred Songs of the Hula*[18] records the use of *hinahina kū kahakai* in *lei:*

Aia i Waimea ku'u kahu lei
Hui me ka wai 'ula 'iliahi
Mōhala ka pua i ke one o Pāwehe
Ka lawe a ke Ko'olau
noho pū me ka ua pūnonohu 'ula i ka nahele
'ike i ka wai kea o Makaweli
ua noho pū ka nahele
me ka lei hinahina o Makali'i

My wreath maker is there at Waimea
Where one meets with the water reddened
    like the *'iliahi* buds.
The flowers bloom on the sands of Pāwehe,
Borne upon the Ko'olau winds.
Dwelling with the red glowing rain in the forest
The white waters of Makaweli are seen
Also dwelling in the forest
With the *hinahina* wreath of Makali'i.
—K. M.

Alohalani Paleka Gomard, Anahaki, Moloka'i

Kolo ka hinahina i ke one kea
Hulali ka lau hina i kāhi panoa
Paoa ke onaona o ka pua
Ke ulu mau nei i kēia one hānau

The *hinahina* crawls on the white sand
Silvery leaf glistening in parched wilderness
The fragrance of the flower is delicate
Growing profusely on these birthing sands   —P. K. K.

Hīnano
Pandanus tectorius

Hīnano is the male inflorescence of *hala*. The flowers are small, white, and fragrant, arranged in a series of fluffy tubular clusters accompanied by white, papery bracts. It is primarily the bracts that are collected by the *lei* maker.

The amusing story of Puapualenalena, a very clever dog, is recorded in a classic *hula* called *"Hula 'Īlio,"* the dog *hula*. Dancers portray, in doglike motions, the activities of this famous canine.[18] The story involves the repeated theft of the king's *'awa* roots by

Ualani Kalaniopi'o, Lālāmilo, Hawai'i

Hīnano
Pandanus tectorius

Puapualenalena, who delivers them to his grateful master. The theft would be deserving of the death penalty. The dog is apprehended but gains the king's forgiveness by successfully stealing a sacred conch shell, previously stolen by the god Kāne, who, after drinking too much *'awa*, greatly disturbed the king by blowing it noisily. The dog returns the conch shell to the appreciative king. Puapualenalena is honored and, in the *hula* version, is rewarded with a *lei hīnano*.[18] Dog and owner live happily ever after. (See also reference 21.)

This charming story offers a small insight to the Hawaiian sense of humor and a welcome relief from the number of serious accounts of the *hālau hula*, the sometimes questionable behavior of gods and goddesses, and of *kauwā* (slaves, outcast class) and human sacrifice. Hawaiians, though frequently serious, are fun loving. Masters of double entendre, they are quick to respond to an off-color reference. The word *"kolohe"* —mischievous, naughty—is commonly applied to actions of less than serious intent.

Malia Akau with dog Tita, Waimea, Hawai'i

No ka hīnano
'O ko'u hoa aumoe ia
E hone mau ana a'i ka mana'o
E nāueue mai ko kino
'A'ole a koe aku ē

The *hīnano,* my night companion
A melodic call constant on the mind
For you to bring hither your body
Until all else cease to exist
—*P. K. K.*

'Ie'ie
Freycinetia arborea

In moist places on all the Islands, except Kaho'olawe and Ni'ihau, the climbing stems of *'ie'ie* cling to forest trees and sometimes scramble over ridges and exposed slopes. They are readily noticed at low elevations and up to 4,500 feet, especially when bearing their large, spectacular, red and orange inflorescences. *'Ie'ie,* associated with Laka, goddess of *hula,* was one of the plants placed on the *kuahu hula.* The brilliant bracts surrounding the flowering cylinder provide the source for a dramatic *lei.*[48] The legend of Pele and Hi'iaka records Pele fashioning a *lei 'ie'ie* while visiting Lāna'i.[19]

The prayer on the right cites a ceremonial use of *'ie'ie:*[18]

Ki'eki'e ka 'ie'ie i Hualālai
Ke ho'ohei a'e nei ka pua pala 'ehu
I 'ōpe'ape'a i kona lele pō'ana
Ola ka 'ie'ie i ka hui 'ana o lāua

The *'ie'ie* is elevated on Hualālai
Its yellow red flower is enticing
The bat during his night flight
By chance they meet,
The *'ie'ie* lives!   —*P. K. K.*

(PULE KUAHU)
E ho'oulu 'ana i kini o ke Akua
Ka lehu o ke Akua
I ka puku'i o ke Akua
I ka lālani Akua
Ia ulu mai o Kāne
Ulu o Kanaloa
Ulu ka 'ōhi'a, lau ka 'ie'ie
Ulu ke Akua, noho e ke kahua
A a'ea'e, a ulu, a noho kou kuahu
Eia ka pule la, he pule ola

(HUI)
E ola ana oe!

(ALTAR PRAYER)
We are inspired by the 40,000 gods
By the 400,000 gods
The 4,000 gods
In the assembly of gods
In the rows of gods
Inspired by Kāne,
Inspired by Kanaloa;
The *'ōhi'a* and leafy *'ie'ie* grow,
Inspired by the gods and resting on the platform,
Rising up and growing, sitting upon your altar.
Here is the prayer, a prayer for life.

(CHORUS)
You shall have life!
—*K. M.*

As part of the ceremony involved in canoe making, a *lei 'ie'ie* was placed on the felled *koa* tree selected for a canoe.[48] *'Ie'ie* is also sacred to Kū, god of war. Boughs and blossoms were used to decorate the war temple.[48]

Ekikiela Chong, Waimea, Hawai'i

'Iliahi
Santalum haleakalae

Four different *'iliahi* species plus several varieties of sandalwood trees are endemic to the Hawaiian Islands. One variety from Lāna'i is endangered. They grow in dry to wet forests from the seashore to high elevations. Once plentiful, sandalwood was heavily harvested by commoners for the chiefs from 1791 to 1840, when the supply of suitably sized, accessible trees was exhausted. The highly fragrant wood was shipped to China, where it was prized for use in producing chests, boxes, and fans. Sandalwood oil was extracted for perfume and medicine. Hawaiians used *'iliahi* to perfume *kapa* and were familiar with the strong fragrance both of the wood and the flowers.

The *'iliahi* pictured is a species from the slopes of Haleakalā, where it is found in dry, alpine scrub at elevations between 5,000 and 8,000 feet. The flowers, though not strongly fragrant, provide the *lei* maker with brilliant red flower buds, *liko* (leaf buds), and flowers.

Kainoa Bargarmento,
Kula, Maui

Ua pi'i ke ahi o loko
Kau ka hali'a a kāua
Wahī i ke kapa ho'okahi
Lilo i ke 'ala 'iliahi

The fire within is kindled
When fond memories arise
Of you and me enveloped as one
Lost in the intoxicating fragrance of *'iliahi*
—*P. K. K.*

'Iliahialo'e

Santalum ellipticum

An endemic plant, the coastal sandalwood *'iliahialo'e* is a variant of a more common species, one of four recognized species that are trees. *'Iliahialo'e* grows on most of the main Islands, along rocky coasts close to sea level and up to lowland ridges often exposed to strong salt winds and subjected to periods of extreme drought. A spreading, dense shrub usually 2 to 3 feet tall, it produces chartreuse flowers, purplish tinged *liko,* and almost succulent gray silvery foliage, all of which make the plant attractive to the *lei* maker.

Ke kolo la ka 'iliahialo'e
I ka 'ehu kai o Kīlauea
Pali uka o Ke'awa'ula

The *'iliahialo'e* creeps upward
At the misty sea of Kīlauea
On the cliff upland of Ke'awa'ula
—*P. K. K.*

Palakiko Apiando, Makapu'u, O'ahu

'Ilima
Sida fallax

'Ilima, found throughout Hawai'i on all the main Islands, as well as on other Pacific Islands and westward to China, is extremely variable in height, flower color, and leaf size and shape. In areas exposed to onshore, salty winds, it grows as a prostrate ground cover (*'ilima kū kahakai*). Inland at higher, somewhat dry elevations, it may be a large shrub up to 5 feet tall, while in wet forest, where it is rarely found, it may be collected at elevations from near sea level to as high as 5,000 feet. Flower color ranges from light yellow (*'ilima hālenalena*) to strong orange-yellow (*'ilima melemele*) and to a bronze red (*'ilima 'ula'ula* or *'ilima koli kukui*). The base of each petal is sometimes marked with dark maroon.[30]

In 1819, French botanist Charles Gaudichaud recorded the collecting of *'ilima* in Kailua, Kona, and its use in *lei*.[25] This is the earliest modern written record of *'ilima* in *lei* making and, perhaps, for the making of *lei* in Hawai'i. *Lei 'ilima*, of course, had been noted in the ancient myth of Pele and Hi'iaka, as later recorded and translated by Nathaniel B. Emerson.[19] (See also reference 30.)

Scottish botanist James Macrae in 1825 noted the presence of a native plant, *'ilima*, growing in the wild areas behind the village of Lāhainā, on Maui. Its bright golden-yellow flowers were collected by *lei* makers.[47]

'Ilima, poetically called *pua 'āpiki*, was at one time planted around houses to have flowers at hand for making *lei* and for medicinal purposes. The term "*'apiki*" means mischievous, as it was believed that a *lei 'ilima* attracted mischievous spirits.[54]

When an *ali'i nui* (high chief) visited an area, it was the joy of the women to gather the small, fragile *'ilima* flowers, *maile* vines,

I ke alaula, aia lā
I ke kai po'i, aia lā
I ka lima o ka lapa'au
'O ka 'ilima ia pua kupainaha

The flower is found in the sunset,
In the breaking waves,
In the flying bird, and
In the healer's hand.
'Ilima is that remarkable flower
—*P. K. K.*

and orange red fruit of the *hala* to make welcoming *lei* to present to the visiting *ali'i.* The *lei* were deferentially placed on the outstretched hands of the royal visitor.[30]

A scene from the epic tale of Pele and Hi'iaka depicts a tragic episode and mentions *lei 'ilima:* after Hi'iaka's departure from Kaua'i with Lohi'au, Pele's "intended," she landed at Ka'ena and proceeded along the arid coast to Mākua. There she caused a cave to open. It provided fresh water. The cave and surrounding area are known as Keawa'ula.[55] Nearby, at a place called Kīpuka-kai-o-Kīlauea, the people, many adorned with *lei 'ilima,* were engaged in a sport called *lele kawa* (leaping or diving into the sea). One beautiful young woman, wearing *lei 'ilima,* jumped into the sea and was killed by hitting a large, supernatural rock, which appeared to have thrust itself into her path.[41] After joining the people in a feast, Hi'iaka proceeded into the mountains to Pōhākea.

In some areas during *kalo* (taro) planting, *lei* of *'ilima, hala,* and *maile* were worn by workers in the *lo'i kalo* (irrigated terrace for growing *kalo*), who dressed in traditional white *malo.* Lines of weeders, mulchers, and planters thus adorned moved forward in unison to the tempo of special *hula* chants.[30]

Lei 'ilima were preferred by Queen Emma over all other *lei.* Perhaps this is what gave rise to the incorrect notion that a *lei 'ilima* was "royal," to be enjoyed only by high chiefs.[30]

Noelani Iokepa,
Keawa'ula, O'ahu

Ipu
Lagenaria siceraria

Ipu, a kind of gourd, is a Polynesian introduction possibly originating in tropical Africa or Asia. This wide-spreading vine is widely grown throughout the tropical Pacific. Its ripe fruit, hollowed and dried, provides the base for fashioning containers of many sizes and shapes, the largest growing to as much as 4 feet long and a foot in girth.

People of the *kauwā* (slave, outcast) class, a despised segment of the traditional Hawaiian population, were forced to live in special ghettolike areas without contact with other classes of Hawaiians. They were permitted to marry only other *kauwā*. Should

forbidden alliances be made with non-*kauwā*, the child of such contact would be put to death. Should a non-*kauwā* even walk on a *kauwā* reservation, knowingly or not, that person was considered defiled and either cleansed or put to death. If no appropriate law-breaker or war victim was available for human sacrifice in the *heiau*, the *kahuna* (priest) was privileged to go to the boundary of the *kauwā* land and select a *kauwā* for the ritual. The *kauwā* could not refuse and was obliged to leave the reserve and obediently follow the *kahuna*. If the sacrifice was not to

Hokulani Lasalio, Kawaihae, Hawai'i

E naki'i ka hue ma ka 'ā'ī
He lei 'olo
He hō'ailona o ka po'e kauwā
He kaumaha no ke kauwā ha'alele loa

Tie the gourd about the neck
It is a gourd *lei*
Symbolic of the anathema
A burden for the outcast   —*P. K. K.*

take place immediately, the *kauwā* was obliged to wear a special *lei*, which was an elongated gourd suspended by a string around the neck and known as the "garland for waiting" (*lei i ke 'olo*); it marked the wearer as a *kauwā* soon to die. This person was shunned, and no Hawaiian would chance any contact with the condemned, risking certain punishment.[5] (See also references 6 and 37.) With the overthrow of the *kapu* system, in 1819, the *kauwā* restrictions came to an end.

Kāmakahala

Labordia degeneri

The small, golden-yellow to orange flowers of several of the fifteen species of the genus *Labordia* are called *kāmakahala*. They are endemic to moist, upland areas on several of the Hawaiian Islands and were highly prized for fashioning into *lei*.[24] Usually shrubby or small trees, one species is a sprawling, vinelike shrub. On Kaua'i, *lei kāmakahala* was not worn by commoners but was reserved for the adornment of *ali'i nui*.[31] (See also reference 16.)

Ka pua o kāmakahala
Ka punihei o ka mana'o
Mea'ole ke ana 'iliwai
Ka loa a me ka laulā
A loa'a 'oe ia'u
Ka pū'ili a ka pu'uwai

The flower *kāmakahala*
Ensnares my thoughts
Surveying the land is nothing to me
Its breadth and width I will travel
Until I have you
For I am the one who will hold you to my heart
—P. K. K.

Namahana Wong, Hanalei, Kaua'i

33

Kamani

Calophyllum inophyllum

Introduced by Polynesians during the early period of immigration to the Hawaiian archipelago, *kamani* is a broad-crowned tree that may reach 60 feet high. It thrives in moist lowland and coastal areas, producing a fine wood and beautiful, white, highly fragrant flower clusters. The dense, tough wood was used to fashion boats, and the flowers for making a delicate *lei*[16] and for perfuming stored *kapa*. *Kamani* is native to the broad area from eastern Africa to India, and to the Tuamotos of French Polynesia. It has become sparingly naturalized in Hawai'i. The wood is carved to make calabashes, and an oil is expressed from the fruits. All parts of the tree have medicinal properties.

Keala Recaido, **lei** *with* **kupukupu,** *Waimea, Hawai'i*

Kāmanu'ia ka manu	The bird was snared
E ke kanaka po'o kamani	By the bald man
Ma luna o ke kumu lā'au	On the *kamani* tree
kamani	—P. K. K.

The poem reproduced above is a beautiful example of good traditional Hawaiian composition, which often involves a clever play on words to convey a double meaning. In this example, the play involves the word *"kamani,"* the name of the tree featured. *Kamanu* is another name for the tree. *"Ka manu"* means "the bird." *"Kanaka po'o kamani"* therefore can be read as referring to a bald man, because the wood, when polished, is tan and pinkish, much like the head of a bald man. The play on words is between the bird, the bald man, and the two names of the same tree; each line focuses on the tree in a different way. (Explanation courtesy of Pualani Kanahele.)

Hokulani Spencer with **lei palai**, *Puakō, Hawai'i*

Kauna'oa

Cuscata sandwichiana

Kauna'oa (dodder), a parasitic vine, is endemic to Hawai'i. It is found in coastal habitats on all the main Islands except Kaho'olawe.

Uncounted ages ago, Pele's epic voyage from Kūkulu-o-Kahiki to the Hawaiian archipelago temporarily effected her escape from her older sister, Nāmaka-o-Kaha'i, the sea goddess. Pele and her company of gods and goddesses worked their way southeast down the long chain of reefs and shoals to Nihoa and eventually to a nearby small islet, where Pele was moved to crown the islet with a *lei kauna'oa*.[19] Hi'iaka placed her *lei lehua* on the islet, thereby giving the islet its name: Lehua Island. Pele's voyaging party

included Kuku'ena, whose duty it was to prepare the *'awa* and to make *lei,* two daily responsibilities of the highest order (see p. 69). *Kauna'oa* is the first of many *lei* recorded in the myth of Pele and Hi'iaka.

The same myth later recounts Hi'iaka, Pele's beloved youngest sister, landing at O'ahu on her return voyage from Kaua'i to Hawai'i. Hi'iaka and her fellow travelers stop on O'ahu at Pu'uloa. Hi'iaka bids her companions to make a *lei kauna'oa*.[19] (See also reference 41.)

Pohihihi ē, pohihihi
Ke kolo hele wale a ke kumu lā'au 'ole
Kolia a mālo'elo'e a heia
Ke one wali o Kauna'oa

Baffling, baffling indeed
How the rootless one crawls about
Pulling until taut and ensnaring
The fine sands of *Kauna'oa*   —P. K. K.

Mahealani Cazimero,
Waimā, Hawai'i

Makeo, Kanehekili, and Kalani Kahoʻopiʻi with lei lāʻī,
ʻUpolu, Hawaiʻi

Kī

Cordyline fruticosa

A Polynesian introduction, *kī* has long been cultivated and has spread wherever people have migrated throughout the Pacific. In contemporary Hawai'i, the name *"kī"* is commonly referred to as "ti." The plant's origin is thought to have been Southeast Asia, from the tropical areas of the Himalayas to Australia. A lowland plant, common in moist areas from the coast up to 1,800 feet, *kī* has many uses: by *lei* makers in forming *lei* and also *pū'olo* (a bundle in which to carry *lei*); for thatching; in cooking to wrap and serve food; and for fashioning sandals and skirts.

A *lei* of *kī* leaves, usually expressed as *lā'ī*, a contraction of *"lau"* (leaf) and *"kī,"* is a simple open or closed *lei* worn around the head, or around the neck or wrists.[28] It carried great powers in protecting the wearer.[18] Priests wore a headband of *kī* leaf, as well as a long, open *lei* of *kī,* which symbolized the power of the priesthood and enacted protection against evil. A woman in menses wore a *lei lā'ī*,[5] and a woman attending her also wore a *lei lā'ī* to protect against defilement.[30] A branch of the *kī* plant was an emblem of peace and was also used to signal a proposal of peace.[17] The delicate blossoms of *kī* were sometimes mixed with other blooms to make an unusual *lei*.[16] (See also reference 36.)

Ho'oheno ho'i ka lā'ī
Kāhili akula i ka ma'i

The ti leaf is cherished
It sweeps away illness
—*P. K. K.*

Kō
Saccharum officinarum

Kō, sugarcane, is another important plant carried to Hawai'i during the period of migration. It has been widely cultivated in tropical Asia and New Guinea since ancient times. Central New Guinea is possibly its original home. Besides its obvious attraction as a sweetener, *kō* was used by *kāhuna* (priests, or experts in any field) in various medicinal applications, and the foliage for thatch. The plumelike flowering stalk is what interests the *lei* maker.[66] *Kō* flowers appear in the fall, usually November, and are silvery white. *Lei* are fashioned from the long flower tassels.

Kō a ke kō kēhau
Ka lihilihi luhi i ka 'ehu
'O ka 'ehu kai ho'okāhiko mai
Ku'u lei 'ōlinolino i ka lā

Sugarcane tassels supporting the dew
Its tassels drooping in the morning
It is the morning mist that bedazzles
My *lei* glittering in the sun
—P. K. K.

Left: Palikiko Apiando with lei hala, *Kahuku, O'ahu*
Right: Johnston Kalawa, Hāmākua, Hawai'i

Koa
Acacia koa

oa may grow to 100 feet tall and is often dominant in dry to wet forests at a wide range of elevations between 200 and 6,000 feet on all the Islands except Ni'ihau and Kaho'olawe. The largest of the native forest trees, *koa* was the hardwood of choice for making canoes, religious images, spears, calabashes, and other hard-use articles.

The word *"koa"* means brave, bold, fearless, and, by extension, a warrior, a fighter. In South Hawai'i and Maui, a bough of *koa* was added to the *kuahu hula* dedicated to Laka, goddess of *hula*, to make *hula* dancers fearless.[4] The foliage was fashioned into a *lei*[18] to be worn by a dancer to eliminate stage fright.[7]

Keoni Visaya, Pu'ukapu, Hawai'i

Lilo ke kumu lā'au koa i wa'a kea
Lilo ke koa pono i 'aumakua
Lilo ka lau koa i lei hoaka
He kāhiko no ke akua

The *koa* log became a spirited canoe
The righteous warrior became a god
The *koa* leaves became a crescent *lei*
An adornment for the god
—*P. K. K.*

Koai'a

Acacia koaia (Acacia koa)

Closely akin to *koa, koai'a* is a rare, much smaller tree found in rather dry habitats on Moloka'i, Lāna'i, Maui, and Hawai'i. Its creamy yellow flowers, which grow arranged in clusters, are fragrant. Both flowers and foliage attract the *lei* maker.

Pōpō ke koai'a pua o uka
Nā hene wai 'olu o Kohala
He hālulu kai puni i ia pua
Ka mumuhu a ka nui nalo meli
Na wai e pakele mai
I ke kīko'o a ka 'ālelo pōka'a?

The ball-like flower of the *koai'a*
Of the gentle slopes of Kohala
A buzzing surrounds this flower
It is the work of swarming honeybees.
Who will rescue this flower
From the darting of reeling tongues?

—P. K. K.

Kehaulani Marshall,
Kawaihae-uka, Hawai'i

Koali

Ipomoea cairica

Koali is found throughout Hawai'i in both dry and wet areas from near sea level to 2,000 feet. It is one of several species of morning glory, which includes the important food plant *'uala* (sweet potato). *Koali* is native to tropical Africa and Asia and is possibly a Polynesian introduction. Gaudichaud recorded its presence in Hawai'i in 1819.[25]

From the early days of the migration period, new settlers in Hawai'i developed a level of engineering and building skills unrivaled throughout Polynesia. One skill stands above all others: the planning, grading, and construction of terraces for growing wetland taro, which involved the collecting and conducting of water from major water sources in the mountains to the growing areas at lower elevations.[44] (See also reference 1.)

Every water conductor, or *'auwai*, whether a small ditch or a large aqueduct, was part of an intricate irrigation system that could mean the difference between feast or famine. The completion of a new water source, a triumph therefore, was occasion for ceremony and celebration. The workers who had successfully demonstrated their skills collected three commonly available materials with which to fashion special *lei* for the occasion: *koali* (a species of morning glory vine), leaves of *mai'a* (banana), and *neke*, a native fern growing in very wet places.[30]

Kalikokauaikekai Hoe with lei mai'a, Waiāhole, O'ahu

No ku'u lei hihi a'ela
He paukū na'u ko'u pono
I pōhai ke po'o i ke koali
Lahilahi i ka pā kakahiaka
Eia lā i ka ho'opōhai
He koali pua hi'ipoi'ia

My *lei* is an ever-climbing vine
I pinch off a section that meets my need
So my head is crowned by *koali*
Blossoms delicate in the morning
Here it circles my crown
The morning glory most cherished
—*P. K. K.*

Koki'o

Kokia drynarioides

In the early days of the agricultural field systems of Kona, *koki'o* was cultivated for its large, brilliant red flowers and for its bark, from which an important dye was derived.[57] Now a rare and endangered species, the endemic *koki'o*, a small tree, is still readily cultivated. It prefers elevations between 1,000 and 2,000 feet in fairly dry situations that reflect its native habitat in North Kona.

Note: Flowers used in making the *lei* pictured were collected entirely from cultivated plants.

'O wai kēlā pua aloalo o uka
Me ka lihilihi huli hope, huli mua?
'O koki'o nō ia
Ka pua lehiwa o ke kula

Who is that upland hibiscus
With petals turning backward and forward?
Indeed, it is *koki'o*
The eye-catching flower of the arid leeward forest
—*P. K. K.*

Peneku Ka'ae, Waimea, Hawai'i

Koki'o Ke'oke'o

Hibiscus arnottianus subsp. *punaluuensis*

Kaua'i, O'ahu, and Moloka'i host several species of the endemic white hibiscus; some species grow as small trees and others as large shrubs. All are beautifully fragrant in the morning hours and last two days without water after picking. The *koki'o ke'oke'o* pictured is closely related to the Tantalus white hibiscus. It is endemic to the area from Kaipapa'u, in upper Moanalua Valley, and the mountains behind Waiāhole, O'ahu, at elevations between 600 and 2,100 feet. This plant thrives in high-rainfall areas, where it grows into a 30-foot tree.

One early botanist noted Hawaiians' predilection for members of the hibiscus family,[25] and another noted their general attraction to fragrant plant materials.[5] Both red and white hibiscus were cultivated by Hawaiians "for sake of their flowers" and also for medicinal purposes.[30] One source specifically cites hibiscus as a *lei* material.[8]

Ku'ulei Feliciano, lei *with* palai, *and* lei hala, *Kalōpā, Hawai'i*

46

Koki'o 'Ula

Hibiscus kokio

Found on all the main Islands except Ni'ihau and Kaho'olawe, *koki'o 'ula* grows as a shrub or small tree at low to medium elevations in dry to wet forests between 200 and 3,000 feet elevation. It bears flowers varying in color from the usual intense red to orange red and sometimes yellow. The blossoms may be used to fashion a bright *lei,* which lasts but one day.[8] To avoid confusion with its close relative noted above, also called *koki'o,* we are referring to this *koki'o* as *"koki'o 'ula."* Although *koki'o 'ula* is not blessed with fragrance, its brilliant flowers are a major attraction to the *lei* maker. It was one of the few species Hawaiians traditionally planted around their dwellings for its flowers.[30]

Nani Bargarmento,
Waiehu, Maui

47

Kōlea Lau Li'i

Myrsine sandwicensis

An endemic shrub or small tree found on O'ahu, Moloka'i, Maui, and Hawai'i, *kōlea lau li'i* may reach 20 feet high. It flourishes in a wide range of habitats, from semi-dry to rain forest and even bogs, at elevations between 1,000 and 3,000 feet. *Lei* makers prize its bright yellow *liko,* which is strongly tinged with red or purple. (See photographs in *lei pāpahi* section, p. 66.)

Kolokolo Kahakai

Vitex rotundifolia

A beach plant found in Hawai'i and throughout the tropical Pacific and Indian Ocean areas, *kolokolo kahakai* has become popular as a cultivated species for beachside gardens. Growing to 3 feet in cultivation, it spreads widely over sand dunes or in soil, rooting at the nodes and thereby making it valuable as an excellent ground cover for erosion control. It is salt, wind, and drought tolerant and has gray green, aromatic foliage. Branch tips bear bright bluish-violet flowers. The flowers and foliage alike are used by the *lei* maker. On Lāna'i, *kolokolo kahakai* is known as *mānewanewa.*[38]

Kapu Kinimaka-Alquiza and Tommy Tokioka, Anahola, Kaua'i

Ko'oko'olau

Bidens menziesii subsp. *filiformis*

Ko'oko'olau species, which take the form of small to medium shrubs, are distributed on all the major Islands, some restricted to but one island or a portion of one island. Certain species may be found in wet areas, others in dry areas, most at low to middle elevations. Some of the nineteen endemic *ko'oko'olau* are prized for their medicinal qualities. *Ko'oko'olau* blossoms may be fashioned into a bright *lei*.[42]

The chant "Hole Waimea" refers to *lei ko'oko'olau* as a "travel wreath," possibly because a traveler in the Waimea area would readily come across *ko'oko'olau* and could easily fashion a *lei* from it.[18] (See also *po'olā nui*, p. 136). One of the many Pele stories tells of her visit to the Kekaha region of Kona "bedecked with *lei ko'oko'olau*."[42]

In the following *mele* (chant),[29] the word "*ko'olau*" (blossom) in the third line is a form of the word "*ko'oko'olau*."

(MELE INOA HULA A KAIONA)
Ua nani ke kula o Kaiona
I ka ho'olai a nā 'iwa.
Kahiko i ka pua ko'olau
He 'ohu kapu no ka wahine.
I kui'ia mai e Li'a.

Beautiful is Kaiona's plain,
Over which the *'iwa* bird poises.
She is bedecked with the *ko'olau* blossom
The adornment that is sacred to her.
It was strung into a wreath by Li'a.

Me he lā ka pua mōhala.
Ho'omāhana 'ana i ka lā
He lā'au maoli ke ko'oko'olau.

The full blossom resembles the sun.
Exuding warmth to the day
The *ko'oko'olau* is a genuine healer.
—*P. K. K.*

50

Kapualikolehuanani Lim with lei 'a'ali'i,
Nalani Holzgrove with lei ko'oko'olau *and*
Kaleimomi Haleamau with lei 'a'ali'i, *'Ōuli, Hawai'i*

Ko'oloa'ula

Abutilon menziesii

From dry places on Lāna'i, East Maui, and Hawai'i, *ko'oloa'ula* is a rare and endangered endemic species inhabiting lowland dry forest habitat up to 1,500 feet elevation. A shrub, it may grow to 6 feet high and is readily propagated and cultivated. Its colorful flowers are favored for *lei*.[29]

Note: Flowers used in making the *lei* pictured were collected entirely from cultivated plants.

Aia i Nāna'i Kaulahea
Ke kui'ia nei ka lei me ka pua laha'ole
'O ke ko'oloa'ula ka nani Lāna'i

There on Lāna'i
The *lei* with the rare flower is being strung
The *ko'oloa'ula* is the beauty of Lāna'i
—*P. K. K.*

Keolikaiaolawemae Texeira,
Kahakuloa, Maui

Kou

Cordia subcordata

A medium-size tree growing to a height of 35 feet, *kou* does best in warm, leeward coastal areas. *Kou* was one of the valuable plants introduced from the south during the period of migration. Its original home probably was Southeast Asia, from where it has been carried throughout the Tropics. *Kou* wood is favored for producing cups, dishes, and calabashes, and its bright orange flowers for making *lei*.[20] The tree's dense foliage provides welcome shade.

In early times, young girls were particularly fond of *lei kou*.[25] A legend involves a young chiefess of 'Ewa, on O'ahu, who angered a *kahuna* by asking for a *lei* of *kou* blossoms being fashioned by the *kahuna*. The *kahuna* summoned sharks, who ate the young chiefess.[53] (See also reference 1.)

Lehualani Pua'ilihau,
Kapuāiwa, Moloka'i

Kou
Cordia subcordata

'O ke kou ka'u
Ko'u pua puāhilo
Ko'u 'ili 'ilima
Ko'u lā'au āuli
Ko'u waiwai Hawai'i

The *kou* is mine
My delicate flower
My *'ilima*-colored petals
My dark wood
My Hawaiian treasure
—*P. K. K.*

Alaonalani and
Lehualani Pua'ilihau,
Kapuāiwa, Moloka'i

54

Kukui
Aleurites moluccana

The *kukui* tree, possibly native to Southeast Asia and introduced during the period of migration, has naturalized on almost all the Hawaiian Islands. *Kukui* displays whitish green, almost luminous foliage in dense, conspicuous groves in moist valleys up to 2,000 feet elevation.

Kukui is valued for many uses: oil, medicinal properties, and as a source of dye. Hawaiians of old fastened *kukui* nuts together and burned them for light, therefore giving the plant its common English name, candlenut. For the *lei* maker, it provides attractive flowers, foliage,[41] and seeds.[1] On Kaua'i, *kukui* flowers and foliage were added to the other plants on the *kuahu hula*.[4] Famous *kukui* groves flourish on Moloka'i, Maui, Kaua'i, and Hawai'i.

Kanani Lindsey with nut lei *and* lei palai, *Pu'ukapu, Hawai'i*

Kukui
Aleurites moluccana

Puhi i ke kukui, ʻikea ka iʻa
Hoʻā i ke kukui, ʻikea ke ala
ʻAʻā i ke kukui, ʻikea ka manaʻo

When the *kukui* is blown, the fish are visible
When the *kukui* is lit, the path is seen
When the *kukui* is aglow, the thought is known —*P. K. K.*

Leonui Rawlins, Kalanikāula, Molokaʻi

Kupali'i
Plectranthus parviflorus

Known as *kupali'i* on Hawai'i, this highly variable species is found from near sea level to 3,000 feet on all the Islands except Kaho'olawe. It is indigenous and also grows across a broad range of other Polynesian areas, Australia, and Southeast Asia. The common English name for *kupali'i* is spurflower.

The *lei* pictured was fashioned from material collected in Kona, where *kupali'i* is a small plant growing in clumps only a few inches high in dry, rocky areas. The small, succulent leaves are gray green and aromatic, and are fashioned into long-lasting, fragrant *lei*.[43] (See also *kūpaoa*, p. 58.)

Kauilani Keakealani, Ka'ūpūlehu, Hawai'i

Kūpaoa
Dubautia scabra

The *kūpaoa* pictured is a small, spreading, mat-forming plant up to 6 inches or so high found at elevations from near sea level to over 6,000 feet on Hawaiʻi, Lānaʻi, Molokaʻi, and Maui. It flowers profusely much of the year, providing a ready supply of clusters of small, white flowers for the *lei* maker.

The word *"kūpaoa"* denotes a strong, permeating fragrance;[54] for *"kūpaoa"*, this refers to using its roots for scenting stored *kapa* and, in earlier times, feather capes.[27] Several closely related yellow-flowered endemic species are referred to as *"kūpaoa"* because of their fragrance. We are using the term *"kūpaoa"* for this white-flowered species to differentiate it from a larger, closely related plant, which we term *"naʻenaʻe."* Both are fragrant, and the two terms are used for both plants.[68]

The "Tradition of Ka-Miki" relates the use of *kūpaoa*, along with *maile, pālai, ʻieʻie, lehua, kupaliʻi,* and *naʻenaʻe,* to make fragrant *lei* for the dedication of a chiefly house and associated gardens.[43] It records that the "entire house was filled with a sweet fragrance beyond compare."

Pomaikalani Bertelmann, lei with kupukupu, *Hualālai, Hawaiʻi*

ʻO ke ʻala kūpaoa kai kūpinaʻi i ka noʻonoʻo
Paʻē holo i ka lipo o ka manaʻo
He ala hoʻi ko kāua e lawea ai
I ka ʻiniki a ke anu kuahiwi
I ka hanu o ka māpu kupaliʻi

The perfume of the *kūpaoa* is echoing in thoughts
A voice striking at the depths of my mind
A pathway to return was provided us
Through the pangs of the cold mountain and
To the wind-borne breath of the *kupaliʻi*
—*P. K. K.*

Kupukupu

Nephrolepis exaltata and *N. cordifolia*

ommon in moist areas throughout Hawai'i from near sea level to 3,500 feet, *kupukupu* is a fern with bold, upright foliage sought by the *lei* maker.[18] Under ideal growing conditions, the fronds may reach 4 feet long. On Maui, it was added to the other materials placed on the *kuahu hula*.[4]

A closely related but smaller plant, sharing the same common name *"kupukupu,"* is also used to make *lei*. It is considerably smaller, with fronds growing to but 2 feet, and is found in high-rainfall areas between 2,000 and 4,000 feet elevation on all the main Islands.

Emerson's *Unwritten Literature of Hawaii: Sacred Songs of the Hula* records *kupukupu* being used to fashion *kūpe'e, lei* worn on wrists and ankles:[18]

Mahoe Pellazar, Waiehu, Maui

(MELE KŪPE'E)
'A'ala kupukupu ka uka o Kāne-hoa
E ho-ā
Hoa nā lima o ka makani, he Wai-kōloa
He Wai-kōloa ka makani anu Līhu'e
'Ālina lehua i kau ka 'ōpua
Ku'u pua
Ku'u pua i'ini e ku-i a lei
Inā iā'oe ke lei 'a mai lā

(ANKLET SONG)
The uplands of Kānehoa are fragrant with the
        kupukupu.
Bind on the *lei.*
Bound on by hands that move swiftly like the
        wind, Waikōloa.
Waikōloa is the cool wind of Līhu'e.
Lehua blemished where the *'ōpua* clouds settle.
My blossom,
My blossom with which I desire to make a *lei.*
If only you were the *lei* that I could wear.   —*K. M.*

Kupukupu
Nephrolepis exaltata and *N. cordifolia*

Lē'ī' ke kupukupu
Mai kuahiwi a i kai
Kuhi ka manamana i ka lani
Pa'a ka manamana i ka honua
Ulu mau nō ma kēia pae 'āina

The *kupukupu* is abundant
From the mountains to the sea
The fingers point skyward
The toes firmly planted in the ground
It grows profusely on all our Islands
—*P. K. K.*

Pa'ola Chandler, Kē'ē, Kaua'i, with **N. exaltata** *lei*
Haunani Kanuha, Pu'ukapu, Hawai'i, with **N. cordifolia** *lei*

Laua'e
Microsorum spectrum

Frequently called *"pe'ahi"* on other Islands, this beautiful fern was traditionally known as *laua'e* on Kaua'i. It grows abundantly there in the high rainfall areas of the Wainiha Pali and west to the precipitous Kalalau Valley, where it may be found from the lowlands up to 2,500 feet. Under ideal conditions, the large, highly fragrant *laua'e* leaves may reach 2 feet long and are highly prized for making *lei.* On Kaua'i, *laua'e* was added to the other plants on the *kuahu hula* dedicated to Laka.[4] It is featured in many chants and *mele.*[50] Makana and Kalalau, on Kaua'i, were noted for the growth and fragrance of *laua'e* ferns. (See also reference 16.)

In the epic myth of Pele and Hi'iaka, as the latter departs Hā'ena with Lohi'au she makes the following farewell address to the precipitous cliffs of Kalalau "and to the deity therein enshrined."[19]

O Ka-lalau, pali 'a'ala ho'i, e
Ke ako ia a'e la e ka wahine;
'A'ala ka pali i ka laua'e e,
I Hono-pū, Wai-aloha.
Aloha 'oe lā, e-e!

The cliffs of Kalalau are indeed fragrant,
Where the woman picks greenery.
The cliffs are made fragrant by the *laua'e,*
There at Hono-pū and Waialoha
Aloha [love] to you there!
—K. M.

Kahu Chandler and
Haleakahauoli Wichman with lei palai,
Limahuli, Kaua'i

Laua'e
Microsorum spectrum

Considerable confusion surrounds the fern popularly known as *"laua'e"* (*Phymatosorus grossus*), which is used extensively in contemporary landscapes, table decorations, and *lei*. The traditional Hawaiian name *laua'e* has been applied to that fern, which was introduced to Hawai'i after 1900. Its growth habit is similar to the true *laua'e*, and it is sometimes quite fragrant. Thriving under a wide range of conditions, it quickly spread throughout Hawai'i and now is commonly but incorrectly thought to be native. (See also references 1, 2, 50, and 71.)

Mahealani Cazimero with **lei hala** *and* **laua'e**,
Kawaihae, Hawai'i
Left: John Mahi, Mā'alaea, Maui

Aia ka laua'e o Makana i uka
Loa'a ka hala 'ula i kai
Huipū'ia e Iponoenoelaua'e i Hā'ena
Ka makani ki'i wahine o Lohi'auipo

The *laua'e* of Makana is upland
The *hala 'ula* is seaward
The duo are united by
Iponoenoelaua'e of Hā'ena
The female-fetching wind of Lohi'auipo

—*P. K. K.*

Lehua 'Āhihi
Metrosideros tremuloides

*L*ehua 'āhihi grows only on O'ahu, at low elevations and up to 2,000 feet in the Ko'olau and Wai'anae mountains. This delicate, slender 'ōhi'a was formerly abundant in the vicinity of the Nu'uanu *pali* and was highly desirable for making *lei.*[20] It grows as a shrub or small tree, occasionally as much as 15 feet tall, with a somewhat weeping habit.

The first verse of Queen Lili'uokalani's poignant song *"Aloha 'Oe,"*[16] written in Maunawili in 1877, mentions the beautiful blossoms of *lehua 'āhihi:*

Ha'aheo 'ē ka ua i nā pali
Ke nihi a'ela i ka nahele
E uhai ana paha i ka liko
Pua 'āhihi lehua o uka

Proudly the rain on the cliffs
Creeps into the forest
Seeking the buds
And miniature *lehua* flowers of the uplands

Makaleka Pekelo, **lei** *with* **pala'ā,** *Kāne'ohe, O'ahu*

Lei Pāpahi ✐

The term *"lei pāpahi"* denotes a *lei* design pattern rather than a specific *lei* plant. *Lei pāpahi* display alternating groups of flowers and leaves in a repetitive design.[54] Although many of the *lei* photographs in this publication depict *lei* made with more than one plant or plant part, their design focus is on one major element. We have included here four contemporary *lei,* which are complex in design and demonstrate a traditional *pāpahi* pattern, not featuring any one particular material.[37]

Lei Hualālai mauka is composed of materials that grow on Hualālai in the wet forest zone. Included in the *lei* are *'a'ali'i, 'ōhi'a,* and *'aiakanēnē.*

Pono Awa'a with mixed lei *of* **'aiakanēnē, lehua, 'a'ali'i,** *and* **pūkiawe,** *Hualālai, Hawai'i*

Lei Pāpahi ✐

Lei Kohala mauka comprises materials encountered in the Kohala *mauka* rain forest, an area well known as a rich source for *lei*-making materials. Included in the *lei* are *'aiakanēnē*, *kōlea lau li'i*, *'ōhi'a*, and *'ōlapa*.

Anuhea Bertelmann with mixed lei of kōlea lau li'i, 'ōlapa, lehua *and* palai, *and* Kekoho Bertelmann with lei 'ōhā, *Kohala, Hawai'i*

Lei Pāpahi

Lei-o-Kuku'ena features a series of *lei* representing Kuku'ena, the goddess of *lei* making.

'O Kuku'ena, ke akua kui lei
I ka uka o 'Ōla'a i ka moku lehua
'O Kuku'ena, ke akua
I ka inu hana 'awa no nā wāhine o ka lani

Kuku'ena, the goddess of *lei* making
Is in the upland *lehua* grove of 'Ōla'a
Kuku'ena, the goddess
Who prepares *'awa* for female deities
—*P. K. K.*

In the epic story of Pele and Hi'iaka,[19] Kuku'ena-i-ke-ahi-ho'omau-honua, usually referred to simply as Kuku'ena, was one of the most important of the gods and goddesses in the mythical canoe *Honua-i-ā-kea* during Pele's flight from Kūkulu-o-Kahiki to escape the wrath of Nāmaka-o-Kaha'i. She was the sea goddess and older sister of Pele. Kuku'ena was charged with the important daily tasks of preparing *'awa* and making *lei*. Pictured here is a series of *lei* made from many different flowers and ferns, depicting the range of Kuku'ena's *kuleana* (mandate).

Keleonapua Weller with **lei hala**, **lei palai**, *and* **lei wiliwili**, *Pu'ukapu, Hawai'i*

Kaleonapua Weller with skirt of **lei**, *Pu'ukapu, Hawai'i*

Lei Pāpahi

Top to bottom: nohoanu, nohoanu, lehua ʻopuʻu, *and* lehua muʻo

Lei-o-Poliʻahu is a striking *lei*, a composition primarily of silver and white to commemorate the snow goddess Poliʻahu. Hawaiian mythology features several snow maidens with white mantles, all of exceptional beauty, wit, and wisdom. They were adventuresome and were enemies of Pele, the volcano goddess. Poliʻahu, the best known of the snow goddesses, is clearly visible each year as her dazzling mantle of white turns the great mountain Mauna Kea into a "white mountain."[69]

ʻO Poliʻahu ke kua wahine o ka mauna nui
ʻO kona mau punahele
ʻO ka ʻaʻahu hau ma Mauna Kea
ʻO ka hau poʻi ma Waiʻau
ʻO ka noe lana wale ma Lilinoe
A ka nohoanu lahilahi
Ka pua keʻokeʻo a lū ka poni
A ka lau hinahina
He ʻālana pono na ke akua

Poliʻahu, the goddess of the great mountain
Whose favorites are
The mantle of snow on Mauna Kea
The icy shroud on Waiʻau
The drifting mist on Lilinoe
And the delicate *nohoanu*
That delicate flower with a touch of purple
And glistening silvery leaves
A prescribed offering for the goddess   —*P. K. K.*

Each winter, Poliʻahu emerges from her ever-frozen home in Lake Waiʻau atop Mauna Kea. Scanning the heavens, she notes the southerly retreat of the sun. The days have become shorter, with temperatures dropping to freezing. With a triumphant

70

The term *"lei pāpahi"*
denotes a *lei* design
pattern rather than
a specific *lei* plant.
Lei pāpahi display
alternating groups of
flowers and leaves in
a repetitive design.

Lei Pāpahi

gesture, she blankets the mountaintop with a brilliant mantle of snow and reigns supreme over her domain. The day inevitably arrives, however, when she witnesses the gradual advance of the sun. The days become longer and temperatures slowly climb, until she is forced to take refuge again in her frozen keep, there to bide her time until the sun again retreats to the south.[69]

All elements of the *lei-o-Poli'ahu* are white in honor of the goddess. All are readily available along the eastern segment of the long trail in the saddle between Mauna Loa and Mauna Kea that connects Hilo and North Kona. Traditionally, Hawaiians collected materials at hand for *lei* making. Those pictured here include the following: *nohoanu*, *'ōhi'a* (the white *liko* [newly opened colored leaves] and *mu'o* [leaf buds] are found at high elevations), *pa'iniu*, *pūkiawe*, and a *limu*, a white, sometimes pendant lichen species, 6 to 8 inches long, commonly collected from branches and tree trunks in the area identified with *lei-o-Poli'ahu*. This lichen is also seen in many other areas on other Islands, at high elevations where clouds frequently brush the ground, providing an almost constant source of moisture. We have not been able to locate a Hawaiian name for it. A beautiful *limu*, it adds fine textural contrast to the heavier elements of *lei-o-Poli'ahu*, and has been identified as *Usnea* aff. *australis*. The term *"limu"* is applied equally to plants living under both fresh and salt water (seaweeds) and also to algae, lichens, mosses, and liverworts.

*Kanoelehua Kawai with mixed **lei** of pa'iniu, pūkiawe, nohoanu, lehua and lichen, Pu'u 'Ōma'okoili, Hawai'i*

Limu Kala

Sargassum echinocarpum

A commonly found plant, *limu kala* grows in shallow coastal waters throughout the Hawaiian archipelago, as well as along many other tropical shores.[1] Although gathered primarily for its medicinal properties, it is still eaten today. *"Kala"* carries several meanings: to loosen, to free; to forgive, to pardon.[54] It is this sense of absolution that was sought when *limu kala* was used in ceremonies to drive away sickness and to obtain forgiveness.

In one particular therapeutic ceremony, a person suffering from an illness, whether physical or emotional, or guilt stricken over an unfortunate happening, would fashion a *lei limu kala.* Wearing the *lei,* the person entered the ocean to let waves wash away the *lei,* thereby receiving healing, forgiveness, and release from stress.[28] (See also reference 46.)

Malie Rea, Punalu'u, Hawai'i

Māewaewa i kai pāpa'u
Kahi lei na ka wili a ke au
No wai kahi lei limu kala
I kalakala a ho'i kauwale?

Swaying while anchored in shallow waters
A *lei* at the mercy of the flux and flow of tides
For whom is this *lei* that absolves wrong
And allows the swift return to one's abode?
—*P. K. K.*

74

Mike'ele Mahi,
Pu'uhonua-o-Hōnaunau,
Hawai'i

Limu Pāhapaha
Ulva fasciata

Wiliʻia ka pāhapaha me ka mokihana
He lei ʻāʻī no Kiliʻoe
Ke haʻa la ua kupua nei
I ke kani a ka pahu i Hāʻena

The *pāhapaha* was wound with the *mokihana*
A neck *lei* for Kiliʻoe
She is dancing, this demigod
To the sound of the drum at Hāʻena   —*P. K. K.*

specially abundant on Kaua'i, the edible *limu pāhapaha* is still collected today and prized for its flavor as it was in times past. The plant varies from island to island, and Hawaiians apply several names to this and other *limu*.[1] Found throughout Hawaiian waters, it also grows in many other tropical shallows. *Lei limu pāhapaha* is intimately tied to the island of Kaua'i. Polihale Heiau, a famous temple at Mānā at the northwest coast of Kaua'i, was one of the places from which souls of the dead took their departure into the setting sun. Visitors to Polihale Heiau, a *heiau* dedicated to the god of the ocean, made a *lei limu pāhapaha* to demonstrate that a visit to the area had been made.[22] Legend tells us that the sea goddess Nāmaka-o-Kaha'i introduced this custom.[55]

Keoholani Pa, Polihale, Kaua'i

Limu is a *kino lau* manifestation of the god Kanaloa.

A legend of Kaua'i relates the story of Polihale, chief of Mānā, whose unusually beautiful daughter was wooed, among others, by the god Kū. Polihale rejected all suitors, thereby angering Kū. In retaliation, Kū began killing the chief's people, one by one. Desperate, Polihale invoked and received the aid of the gods Kāne and Kanaloa, whose intervention enabled the people of Mānā to vanquish Kū. To show his gratitude, Polihale built a great five-terraced temple, which was named in his honor.[70] The story of Kawelo tells of Kaleha, who traveled from Kapa'a to Mānā to visit Polihale Heiau. When he reached Mānā, he ornamented himself with *lei pāhapaha* of Polihale.[22] *Lei limu pāhapaha* was used both at Polihale and in Kona for special *hula*.[1]

Mai'a

Musa x *paradisiaca*

Mai'a, banana, has been cultivated for food and fiber for millennia. About thirty-five banana species originate in high-rainfall tropical climates across the broad area from eastern India to the Solomon Islands and south to Australia. These species, through hybridization, have produced many varieties. The Hawaiian *mai'a* derives from hybrids developed in the area centered in Indonesia. Some authorities estimate as many as seventy different kinds of *mai'a* were grown by Hawaiians in pre-contact times. Hawaiian *lei* makers used the leaves for *lei* and also used fibers extracted from the leaf bases of certain varieties. Among other functions, *mai'a* stems and leaves were used in cooking and serving food and in medical applications; the leaves and fruit were used in religious ceremonies. The fruit of most varieties were *kapu* (forbidden) to women.

Several styles of banana-leaf *lei* worn by men are described in detail by the early botanist Gaudichaud.[25] *Mai'a* is associated with the god Kanaloa. The relationship between Kanaloa and the bubbling fresh water, the water of life, is classical. See also *koali* (p. 44) and *'awapuhi* (p. 14) for two other *lei* incorporating *mai'a*.

Kawaiolimaikamapuna Hoe,
Waiāhole, O'ahu

Manomano nā Kanaloa
No Kanaloa-i-ka-wai-pua'i
No moho ke kiu o ka wai ola
I māno wai ka lei lau lau mai'a
Ua kanaloa nā māno wai punapuna

Numerous are the manifestations of Kanaloa
For Kanaloa of the bubbling fresh water
And for Kamohoali'i seeker of this water of life
To channel this water of life, we wear the
    banana-leaf *lei*
Secure are the bubbling springs

—*P. K. K.*

79

Maile
Alyxia oliviformis

Maile is sacred to Laka, goddess of the hula.[18] It is one of the five standard plants that in times past were placed on the *kuahu hula*, the hula altar: *maile* (any form), *ʻōhiʻa lehua* (branch and flowers), *hala pepe* (branch and flowers), *ʻieʻie* (branch with blossom), and *palai*. Other plants also could be added.[4] Dancers were frequently adorned with *lei maile* in honor of Laka. They later draped them on a piece of uncarved wood from the *lama* tree that had been wrapped in yellow *kapa*, representing Laka.[18] This, too, was placed on the altar. The word *"lama"* suggests enlightenment.[54]

The following altar prayer is addressed to Laka:[18]

Haki pū o ka nahelehele,
Haki hana maile o ka wao,
Hoʻoulu lei ou, o Laka, e!
O Hiʻiaka ke kāula nāna e hoʻoulu nā maʻi
A ʻaeʻae a ulu a noho i kou kuahu,
Eia ka pule lā, he pule ola,
He noi ola nou, e-e!

(HUI)
E ola iā mākou, aʻohe hala!

Broken and gathered in the forest
Broken to make the *maile* garland of the wild lands
A garland by which to be inspired by you, Laka!
Hiʻiaka is the seer who grants growth from illnesses,
Rise up and grow, settle upon your altar,
Here is the prayer, a prayer of life,
Our request is for life from you!

(CHORUS)
Grant us life that does not end.
—K. M.

Kikaʻiliʻula Espere and Wiliama Manu,
Kawaihae, Hawaiʻi

80

Kamakele Kailiwai and Kimo Lim,
Kalōpā, Hawaiʻi

Maile
Alyxia oliviformis

E nā poʻe maile
Ka lauliʻi, ka kaluhea, ka haʻiwale, ka pākaha
E hoʻonani ana iā Laka
Īheʻe ko ʻala iā Kūmokuhāliʻi

Say *maile lau liʻi, kaluhea,*
Haʻiwale, pākaha
You honor Laka
Your fragrance prevails through the forest.
—P. K. K.

    Maile, commonly seen as a twining vine, may also be found as a creeping or small, erect shrub. It is endemic and found on all the main Islands except Kahoʻolawe and Niʻihau, growing in sites from near sea level to 6,000 feet and occupying a wide range of habitats, from dry, open sites to high-rainfall areas in deep shade.

Kia Fronda, Waipiʻo, Hawaiʻi

Maile
Alyxia oliviformis

Maile foliage is highly variable in size and shape, as noted in the poem above and seen in the accompanying photographs. Pictured are *maile kaluhea, maile lau li'i,* and *maile lau nui. Maile lau li'i li'i* has very small leaves. All are beautifully fragrant and highly prized. Of the *lei makamae, maile* in several leaf forms is probably the most popular and most readily available today. Legend tells us of the four *maile* sisters, Mailelauli'i, Mailekaluhea, Mailepākaha, and Maileha'iwale, who characterize the variety of leaf shapes and sizes.[20] One of the most favored *lei, maile* is frequently mentioned in legends, chants, and prayers from all the Islands.

Traditionally, men preferred *lei maile* over the more flamboyant flower *lei* and wore them on an almost daily basis.[25] Women, however, also wore *maile,* as well as *lei* made from other materials available in season: "all the fragrant plants, all flowers, even the colored fruits" were collected by the *lei* maker.[25] An account taken from the Pele and Hi'iaka epic describes a woman "completely covered with garlands of *maile lau li'i.*"[41] The notorious Kalelealuakā before his first battle adorned himself with multiple strands of *lei maile lau li'i.*[66]

The gathering chant "Pūpū Weuweu e, Laka E" is highly appropriate here:[40]

Maleko Keli'iholokai, Pu'ukapu, Hawai'i

84

Pūpū weuweu e, Laka e!
O kona weuweu ke ku nei
Kaumaha a'e la iā Laka
O Laka ke akua pule ikaika.
Ua ku ka maile a Laka a imua;
Ua lū ka hua o ka maile.
Noa, noa ia'u, ia Kahaula
Pāpālua noa.
Noa, a ua noa
Eli-eli kapu! eli-eli noa!
Kapu 'oukou, ke akua!
Noa mākou, ke kānaka.

Gather the greenery of Laka
Her greenery stands before us
Laka is worshipped
Laka is goddess of the strong prayer
The *maile* of Laka stands before us
The seeds of the *maile* are scattered
Free, I am free to dream
Twofold freedom
It is opened, it is freed.

Haunani Woolsey, Keawanui, Moloka'i

85

Naleialoha Kunewa with **lei hala**, *Pu'uhonua-o-Hōnaunau, Hawai'i*

Māmane

Sophora chrysophylla

Found on all the main Islands except Niʻihau and Kahoʻolawe, *māmane* is particularly plentiful in high, cold, dry locations on East Maui and Hawaiʻi but also may be encountered in hot areas near sea level. Usually seen as large shrubs or small trees, *māmane* may reach 40 to 50 feet tall. *Māmane* in full flower is a striking sight: bright yellow flowers clustered at branch tips are a foil for the handsome gray-green foliage. The pea-shaped blossoms are gathered for making a beautiful *lei*.[51]

Puou Kunewa, **lei** *with* **palai,**
Puʻuhonu-o-Hōnaunau, Hawaiʻi

ʻO Hiʻiaka-ka-pua-o-ka-māmane
Hoʻopuluʻia e Lilinoe
ʻOhuʻohu nō Mauna a Wākea
He ʻihilani

O Hiʻiaka of the *māmane* blossom
Moistened by the mist of Lilinoe
You adorn the mountain of Wākea
A royal splendor   —P. K. K.

87

Mānewanewa

Vitex rotundifolia

Solomon Kaopuiki, Polihua, Lānaʻi

Mānewanewa (beach vitex)[38] is a spreading, prostrate vine or low shrub growing on the island of Lānaʻi in sand dunes above the reach of the ocean waves. Its gray green foliage is aromatic, its flowers violet blue. On other Islands (except Kahoʻolawe, where it has not been collected), the plant known on Lānaʻi as *mānewanewa* is called *kolokolo kahakai*. Indigenous to Hawaiʻi, it is widespread throughout warm coastal regions from Japan south to Australia and west to the Indian Ocean and to many Pacific Islands.

Polihua, a pristine, broad sandy beach at Kaʻena, on the northwestern end of Lānaʻi, is famed as the legendary site where ʻAiʻai, the fish demigod, marked a stone that became the first Hawaiian *honu* (sea turtle). It is still a famous sea-turtle nesting area. The name literally means "eggs in bosom."[55]

A Lānaʻi tradition involves people making the long, difficult trek to Polihua to witness the annual hatching of turtle eggs and the hatchlings' desperate race across the sand to relative safety in the ocean. A person's proof of having successfully made the arduous journey was the fashioning and wearing of a *lei mānewanewa*.[38] This trek took place during the two months after *honu* nesting, between mid-May and September, when temperatures are suitable for the developing hatchlings.[12]

The *honu* is culturally significant for Hawaiians. Traditionally, sea turtles were symbolic of good luck and long life. For some families, the *honu* was worshipped as an *ʻaumakua*, a family guardian. The *honu* is a *kino lau* form of Kanaloa, god of the sea, which underscores the importance of *mānewanewa* in the tradition.[12] Lines from

an anthem written around 1920 confirm the use of *mānewanewa* as a *lei* plant:
"*Ohuohu Polihua i ka Mānewanewa*
Ka lei kaulana o ka ʻāina
Polihua adorned with *mānewanewa*
The celebrated wreath of the land."[38]

A Nānaʻi Kaʻula ē
Mānewanewa lei kau i ka hano
Hanohano ka umauma ke leia
Ka umauma kapu o kā Wākea

At Nānaʻi, child of Kaʻula
Honored is the *lei mānewanewa*
Magnificent on the chest when worn
On the sacred breast of Wākea's child
—*P. K. K.*

89

Manono

Hedyotis centranthoides

One of several closely related endemics called *"manono,"* the species pictured here is a shrub that grows several feet high, frequently somewhat sprawling or scrambling through other shrubbery. *Manono* is found in moist to semi-dry areas on all the Islands except Niʻihau and Kahoʻolawe, from near sea level to 4,000 feet. It may inhabit open, sunny areas or lightly shaded areas in mixed forest.

Lei makers collect the new growth, which is leathery, glossy, and dark purple. It lasts well in a *lei* and has long been in common usage.

ʻO ka nae o ka manono kaʻu aloha
E kiliʻopu ai i ka lipo nahele
O huli mai, ʻākelekele
I ka papa lauahi o Welawela

The soft fragrance of the *manono* is my love
Calling an invitation to love in the deep forest
Turn to me and let us escape
To the fire flats of Welawela
—*P. K. K.*

Paki Hoʻopai with mixed lei *of* manono, pūkiawe, kūpaoa, *and* kupukupu, *Kīpuka ʻĀinahou, Hawaiʻi*

90

Ma'o

Gossypium tomentosum

An endemic shrub that may grow 6 feet high under ideal conditions, *ma'o* (Hawaiian cotton), is found in arid areas at low elevations, from near sea level to 400 feet, on all the Islands except Hawai'i. Its bright yellow flowers are gathered to make *lei*.[41] One reference describes a *lei pāpahi* with alternating flowers of *ma'o* and *'ilima*.[37] *Ma'o* blossoms are also used to make a beautiful yellow-green dye, and the leaves produce a rich red-brown dye. *Ma'o* foliage is an attractive gray-green, a color foil for the bright yellow blooms.

Ma'o pua o ka lā
He mōhalu ko ka pi'i o ka lā ma Ha'eha'e
He mae ko ka 'aui o ka lā ma ka Hālāwai
Hemolele wale kona nani ke kau i ka lolo ia lā

The *ma'o* blossom is good for a day
A blooming awaits the sun climbing in the east
A wilting awaits the sun setting in the west
Pureness is its beauty when the sun alights
    on high   —*P. K. K.*

Aipolani Makua Nakamura and Kaleialoha 'A'arona-Lorenzo, Kohelepelepe, O'ahu

91

Milo

Thespesia populnea

Whether *milo* is indigenous or another of the migration-period imports has not been decided by botanists. It is native to many tropical coasts from the rim of the Indian Ocean to Melanesia. In Hawai'i, this handsome, useful tree grows throughout the Islands in coastal areas, where it has naturalized. *Milo* may reach 40 feet high. The wood is used to make containers, and the bark and leaves have uses in medicine and for dye, tannin, and oil. But it is the yellow flowers, borne almost year-round, that attract the *lei* maker.[25]

Ke kumu lā'au milo māmalu pono
'Oki ka hua milo, hū ka waiho'olu'u
Milo 'ia ka mo'olelo, lohe ka mele
'Ōmilo ka hau, ō'ili ka milo lopi
Kui nā pua milo, lei ka lei melemele

The *milo* tree, excellent shade,
Cut the *milo* fruit, the dye oozes,
Weave the story, hear the song,
Twist the *hau*, a fine thread appears
String the flowers, wear the yellow *lei*.
—P. K. K.

Malia Makanani, Puakō, Hawai'i

Moa

Psilotum nudum

Hokulani Lasalio, Pu'uhonua-o-Hōnaunau, Hawai'i

*M*oa may be found throughout the Tropics growing on tree trunks, rocks, and even recent lava flows with sufficient moisture. It may reach 2 feet high, forming a bushy mass several feet across. *Moa* is a primitive form of plant life, without true leaves or roots. Though not a true fern, the common English name for it is whisk fern. Hawaiians found several uses for this plant: they brewed a tea from its green stems and used its plentiful spores as talcum powder. The *lei* maker gathered the tufted tips to fashion into a *lei* or to be added to other materials in a mixed *lei*.[45]

Ulu ka moa
I ke kumu lā'au o ka waoakua
I ka 'a'ā laulā
I ka 'ao'ao o ka hāpu'u
Na wai i halihali i ka mea 'a'a 'ole
Pua'ole, ananea?
Na ka makani 'ohi moa o Hawai'i.

The *moa* grows
On the tree trunks of the upper forest
On the expansive lava fields
On the sides of the lower forest tree ferns.
Who transports this rootless,
Flowerless, leafless wonder?
It is the *moa*-gathering wind of Hawai'i.   —*P. K. K.*   93

Mokihana
Melicope anisata

An endemic growing as a shrub or small tree, *mokihana* is highly prized for its strongly anise-scented fruit, which are collected by the *lei* maker.[18] *Mokihana* is fairly common in semi-dry to wet forest areas on Kaua'i at elevations between 1,000 and 3,000 feet. Hawaiians traditionally used it to scent *kapa. Mokihana* is another *lei makamae* still popular and available today. (See also *alani*, p. 13.)

Lawea kāua i ka mokihana
I ka uka o Kōke'e
No ia 'ala a kāua i ho'onipo ai
I ka nahele ā aumoe!

The *mokihana* transports us
To the uplands of Kōke'e,
For its fragrance causes us
To linger in the forest until late.　—*P. K. K.*

Maile Baird *with* **lei maile,**
Holoholokū, Kaua'i

Na'ena'e
Dubautia ciliolata subsp. *ciliolata*

Na'ena'e is a shrub that grows to 5 feet high, bearing bright yellow-orange flowers. It is found only on Hawai'i, usually in very exposed, semi-dry habitats at elevations from 2,700 to over 9,000 feet. The flowers, gathered between June and November, may be used to make a fragrant *lei*.[43]

One of the meanings of the base word *"nae"* is fragrant, sweet smelling. *"Na'ena'e"* denotes fragrance, as in the *na'ena'e* bloom. We have noted in the description for *"kūpaoa"* that both words, *"kūpaoa"* and *"na'ena'e,"* refer to fragrance and are seemingly interchangeable. We are ascribing the name *"na'ena'e"* to this close relative of *kūpaoa,* which grows at lower elevations.[68]

He na'ena'e pua kā kai ala
Lana au i ke au moana
He pua na'ena'e ko uka nei
Lana kau i ka iwi lei o kānaka.

The sea is home to *na'ena'e* school of fish
Floating aimlessly in the currents of the ocean
The *na'ena'e* found on land
Is buoyant on the collar of men   —*P. K. K.*

*Pomaikalani Bertelmann with mixed **lei** of* **na'ena'e** *and* **kūpaoa***, Hualālai, Hawai'i*

Nānū

Gardenia brighamii

Of the three species of endemic gardenias, *nānū*, the one pictured, is a small tree reaching 15 feet tall, which bears single, white, sweetly fragrant blossoms. It is rare and endangered but grows readily in cultivation in hot, semi-dry areas. In the wild, a few *nānū* may still be found at elevations between 1,000 and 1,500 feet on Lānaʻi, Oʻahu, Molokaʻi, and West Maui; a single specimen grows in West Hawaiʻi. *Nānū*, because of its singular fragrance and the purity of the white in its petals, is a favored flower of the *lei* maker.

One account describes the visit of Kamehameha I to Kaunolū on the southeastern coast of Lānaʻi, where he had built a residence. This was one of the king's favored spots for fishing, surfing, and war sports. Upon the arrival of the king, *lei nānū* were placed around the necks of his young warriors, while other *lei* were used to festoon the plaited *pili* thatch of the king's quarters. The king himself was crowned with *lei maile*.[26]

Another, older story relates the death of Puʻupehe, daughter of a lesser chief of Maui. Famed for her great beauty, she was married to Makakēhau, a chief of Lānaʻi. When she met an early, tragic death, her beautiful, lifeless body was wrapped in bright new *kapa* and covered with garlands of fragrant *nānū*.[36]

A more recent account describes a *hula* performance in Lāhainā on July 6, 1823, for Queen Keōpūolani, during which the dancers were wearing *lei nānū*.[17]

Note: The flowers pictured in the *lei nānū* were gathered from a cultivated plant.

Hikoʻula Hanapī, **lei** *with* **palai,**
Moanalua, Oʻahu

'O ka nānū 'a'ala o Nāna'i
E ho'opili ana 'oe me ke oho pili
He lei ali'i no ia

O fragrant *nānū* of Lāna'i
You will be joined with strands of *pili*
And become a chiefly ornament

—*P. K. K.*

Kawamae Andrade, **lei** *with* **pili** *grass,
Kahakuloa, Maui*

97

Naupaka Kahakai
Scaevola sericea

Pi'ilani Smith and Wiliama Manu, Kēōkea, Hawai'i

aupaka kahakai, usually seen as a wide-spreading shrub 5 to 6 feet high, may reach 10 feet tall under ideal conditions. Found along tropical and subtropical coasts in both the Pacific and Indian Oceans *naupaka kahakai* is a common part of the beach flora, flourishing in the teeth of the salt wind. It is drought tolerant and produces roots on contact with sand or soil. The plant forms a dense mass, providing effective protection against wind erosion and making it an active sand dune builder.

Its small, fragrant, white flowers, resembling but half a flower, are patiently strung into *lei*. The soft tip growth and white, spherical fruits may also be used by the *lei* maker. A closely related species, *naupaka kuahiwi (S. gaudichaudiana)* (not pictured) is also used by the *lei* maker.

Naupaka kahakai is said to have been engendered by the gods, as recorded in the history of Kuali'i:[20]

Noho Wākea noho 'ia Papa
Noho 'ia Kanānānu'ukumamao
Hānau ka naupaka, ku i ke kahakai

Wākea lived and took Papa
Lived with Kanānānu'ukumamao
Naupaka was then born, which stands by the
    seashore. *—K. M.*

Hapa pō'aha ka pua ke'oke'o
Me ka ni'o poni, 'o ka naupaka ia
'A'ole he pua maoli i Hawai'i wale nō
No nā mokupuni a pau o Kanaloa.

The white blossom with purple streaks
Appearing as half a flower is the *naupaka*.
Not only indigenous to Hawai'i,
It belongs to all the islands of the great ocean god.
—P. K. K.

Nehe

Lipochaeta lavarum

Twenty species of *nehe* are endemic to the Hawaiian Islands. Some are found in coastal habitats, others in areas to 1,650 feet elevation. Usually growing under dry conditions, the plants vary in form from ground covers to shrubs. All bear attractive bright yellow flowers favored by Hawaiians and used by the *lei* maker.

The *nehe* pictured is a shrub that grows 2 to 3 feet tall, forming dense mounds. It is abundant in the area served by the long, hot, dry trail on East Maui in the rain shadow of Haleakalā running from Kanaio to Nu'u and Kaupō. Plentiful *nehe* flowers illuminate the landscape. This *nehe* is also found in dry sites on Moloka'i, Lāna'i, the northwest coast of Hawai'i, and even Kaho'olawe.

Kaonohiokalā 'Uweko'olani, **lei** *with* **'a'ali'i,** *Waiehu, Maui*

Aia ma ka 'a'ā pōuli o Kanaio
Noho ka po'e nehe
He nānaina 'ōlinolino no ia 'āina

There on the dark *'a'ā* of Kanaio
Sits a group of *nehe*
A dazzling sight for this land
—*P. K. K.*

Neke
Cyclosorus interruptus

A fern occurring in Hawai'i and through-out the tropical Pacific Islands, *neke* is common in freshwater marshy areas, from the coast upland to 1,500 feet.[62] *Neke* spreads by creeping rhizomes, producing foliage that forms a dense ground cover. It grows to 3 feet or more, in full sun or light shade. The stiff, upstanding fronds may be used to create a lush *lei*.[30] *Neke* is sometimes referred to as swamp cyclosorus.

Neke lau pala o ka naele
Neke kapalili po'ohiwi
Me he kīhei ku'uwelu ala 'oe
Hīhīmanu i ka hākilo a ka malihini

The *neke* fern is of the marshland
Neke flutters on the shoulders when worn
    as a *lei*
You are like a tasseled shawl
Elegant to the eyes of the beholder
—*P. K. K.*

Kahikukala Hoe with **lei neke** *and* **lei mai'a,**
Waiāhole, O'ahu

Niu

Cocos nucifera

The coconut, believed to have originated in the Old World tropics, has been planted in tropical areas worldwide. It thrives from moist coastal sites to low forested areas. One of the most important Polynesian introductions, it provided utensils, food, drink, medicine, fiber, and material for thatch and basketry. The coconut palm may reach 100 feet high.

The ivory white flowers of *niu* were prized by the people of Wai'anae for *lei* making. They fashioned head *lei* from *niu* blossoms, and *lei* of *maile lau li'i* from Ko'iahi to wear about the neck.[39]

No ka pua niu kau pōniuniu i luna
Kau keha pōniuniu i ka lani
I ka lima māaniani pōniuniu i ka moa'e
Ko'u lei pāpahi ia na ka lima pa'anehe

As for the coconut flower placed dizzily
    on high
Above all others, dizzy in the heavens
In the tranquil hands, dizzy in the trade winds
My adornment is in the sure hands of the
    lei maker

—*P. K. K.*

Nohoanu

Geranium cuneatum subsp. *hololeucum*

An endemic shrub found in the alpine and subalpine flora of Haleakalā, on Maui, and also on Hawai'i, *nohoanu* thrives in exposed, windswept areas at elevations between 4,000 and 10,000 feet. Its long-lasting, silvery white foliage is a brilliant accent in the landscape, attracting the *lei* maker. White *nohoanu* flowers, sometimes purple-streaked, are also collected for *lei*. This plant is related to the temperate-zone geraniums known collectively as cranesbills. (Photo appears with *lei Poli'ahu*, in *lei pāpahi* section, p. 70)

Palikiko Apiando with **lei maile lau li'i,** *Mākaha, O'ahu*

Nuku'i'iwi
Strongylodon ruber

Nuku'i'iwi, literally "beak of the 'i'iwi," produces a pendant cluster of blossoms as red and curved as the beak of the famed bird. An endemic vine, it grows on Hawai'i, Kaua'i, O'ahu, Maui, and Moloka'i in semi-dry to wet forest areas from 500 to 2,400 feet. Hawaiians cultivated the vine for its flowers. It is sacred to Laka and perhaps to Kapo.[18] The flower, sacred to the gods and to those whom they love, must not be picked and worn by one not loved by the gods, for fear of being haunted by a headless woman carrying her head under one arm.[5] James Macrae's 1825 publication *With Lord Byron at the Sandwich Islands* contains an excellent early drawing of *nuku'i'iwi* from a specimen Macrae collected at Waiānuenue (Rainbow Falls), just *mauka* of Hilo.[47]

Top: Kamu Po'oke'oke'o, Pu'ukapu, Hawai'i
Opposite page: Kekela Ili, lei with 'āwikiwiki, Makapu'u, O'ahu

Aia i leila nuku'i'iwi
I luna loa o ka wao nahele ēulu
Ho'ō i ka nuku kikiwi
I ka piko o ka pua lehua'ula
Aia i leila ka nuku'i'iwi
I luna loa o ka wao nahele ēulu
I lalo iho ka ulu 'ana nā pua iā Haumea
He mau pua 'iu'iu
He lei 'i'ini no nā pua ali'i

The 'i'iwi is there
High in the forest canopy
Dipping its curved beak
Deep into the red *lehua* blossom
The *nuku'i'iwi* is there
High in the forest canopy
Thrusting its blooms earthward
Majestic ornaments
Desired *lei* for royal beings   —*P. K. K.*

'Ōhā
Clermontia kohalae

Kekoho Bertelmann with **lei 'ōhā** *and* **lei 'ōlapa,**
Waimea, Hawai'i

106

Although no clear, written sources for including *'ōhā* as *lei makamae* have come to light, the Kohala District of the Big Island maintains a strong tradition of using the species pictured here. This *'ōhā* inhabits wet forests at elevations between 1,000 and 3,000 feet in the Kohala and Hāmākua Districts of Hawai'i. It forms a large shrub, 6 to 18 feet tall.

There is ample evidence that Hawaiians were aware of the many species closely related to *'ōhā*, a lobeliad, and gave several of them special names, such as *'ōhā wai, 'ōhā wai nui, hāhā 'aiakamanu, 'ōhā kēpau, hāhā nui, hāhā lua'akū'akū, pōpolo, pua kala, 'akū*, and *kuhi'aikamo'owahie*. Hawaiians knew that the leaves and fruit of several kinds were edible and collected them as food;[11] they also valued the highly colorful flowers of these species as lasting for several days after picking. Gaudichaud in 1819 described numerous species of *'ōhā* relatives growing close to habitations on O'ahu.[25] Dr. Franz Meyen in 1831 referred to Gaudichaud's collections of numerous lobeliads in locations readily accessible to Hawaiians and even noted that he had discovered a new species in the same location.[51] In 1919, Joseph Rock deplored the destruction of lowland flora by cattle, specifically lobeliads.[56] *'Ōhā* and its many relatives are endemic, many tragically now extinct. Possibly, given the attraction purple holds for Hawaiians,[64] flowers of many species were collected for *lei*, but this would have had a negligible effect on lobeliad survival.

Mūkī ka 'i'iwi ka wai momona
He 'ono laha'ole ka 'ōhā

The *'i'iwi* sips the nectar of the *'ōhā*
A rare delight
—*P. K. K.*

'Ōhai

Sesbania tomentosa

Formerly widespread at hot, dry, low elevations and along the coast, *'ōhai* is now restricted to small habitat pockets where development and the destruction caused by feral and domesticated animals have not affected its survival. A rare and endangered endemic, *'ōhai* is usually found growing as a low, sprawling shrub on all the main Islands and Necker and Nihoa to the northwest; one form grows into small, erect trees reaching 18 feet high. The flower colors vary widely, from scarlet to salmon to orange red, even yellow. *'Ōhai* blossoms, found most of the year, are prized by the *lei* maker.[35]

The presence of *'ōhai* among the plants of the seashore is explained in Hawaiian legend: the sea goddess Nāmaka-o-Kaha'i carried *'ōhai* to Hawai'i from Kahiki (Tahiti).[18]

Some confusion surrounds the names "*'ōhai*" and "pride of Barbados." Harold St. John records pride of Barbados being introduced into the Islands in 1828.[60] Laura Judd's diary, in an entry dated June 1828, notes that the young King Kauikeaouli (Kamehameha III) had instructed a servant to make a *lei 'ōhai* for her. She adds, in parentheses: "Pride of Barbados."[35] We are certain that this was a later unfortunate editorial addition, possibly made in 1928 when the original text was reprinted in Honolulu, for it would be highly improbable that pride of Barbados flowers were sufficiently plentiful for fashioning a *lei*, given its introduction only six months previously, at most.

Note: Flowers used in making the *lei* pictured were collected entirely from cultivated plants.

Auhea 'oe ku'u wehi
Nēia pua i ke kuni a ka lā
I ka hahana pua wawe o nā kaha
Nā kaha pānoanoa kanaka'ole
I laila kou inoa e ō mai
'O 'oe ka 'ōhai o ke kaha kanaka'ole

If I may beg your attention, my precious,
This crest branded by the sun
In the quick rising heat of the plains
The barren stretch void of humanity
There awaits your name, do answer
You are the *'ōhai* of that place without inhabitants
—*P. K. K.*

Maui   *Moloka'i*

Imehana Mitchell, Mā'alaea, Maui

108

ʻŌhelo
Vaccinium reticulatum

Liliko kaʻōhelo i ke kēhau o uka   The *ʻōhelo* blooms in the mist of the uplands   —*P. K. K.*

Hokulani Kaikaina, **lei liko ʻōhelo** *with* **wāwaeʻiole** *and* **palai,**
Piʻopiʻo, Hawaiʻi

ʻŌhelo, an endemic shrub, is commonly found on Hawaiʻi and Maui and rarely on Kauaʻi, Oʻahu, and Molokaʻi. Growing to 2 feet high as a densely foliated, somewhat scrambling shrub, ʻōhelo thrives at elevations of 1,800 feet to over 10,000 feet. The fruit of the ʻōhelo is harvested to make jams and jellies, or simply to be eaten fresh.[8] But the lei maker gathers many different, colorful parts of this small shrub: the tight clusters of immature fruit, varying in color from light to dark red to orange, sometimes yellow and even pink; the flowers, in clusters, varying from yellow to red; and the liko, similarly variable in color.

A legend tells of Kaʻōhelo, a younger sister of Pele and Hiʻiaka, who lived on Lānaʻi. Before her death, Kaʻōhelo directed her son, Kiha, to bury her at Kīlauea. Instead, parts of her body were distributed to Maui, Oʻahu, Kauaʻi, and Hawaiʻi, where they sprouted into ʻōhelo shrubs. On Lānaʻi, ʻōhelo fruits were strung and worn as lei.[23] Isabela Bird, in 1873, related seeing Hawaiians at Kīlauea Crater stringing ʻōhelo fruit into lei.[8]

Toward the breakdown of the kapu system in Hawaiʻi, Chiefess Kapiʻolani visited Kīlauea Crater in 1824 to defy Pele. Among other actions, the chiefess deliberately ate kapu ʻōhelo, fruit held sacred to Pele.[21]

Pomaikalani Bertelmann, Waimea, Hawaiʻi

111

'Ōhi'a

Metrosideros polymorpha

'Ōhi'a, an endemic species, is found on all the main Islands except Kaho'olawe and Ni'ihau, from near sea level to elevations over 6,000 feet. Extremely variable in form, it may be seen in dense groves as a large tree attaining a height of 100 feet in high-rainfall areas, or as stunted trees scattered singly in dry rain-forest habitats and on recent lava flows. Besides its beautiful flowers, 'ōhi'a displays an amazing variation in the color of its *liko* (newly opened colored leaves), also prized by the *lei* maker.[30] *Liko* may be opaque or translucent red, a grayish lavender, white, or even pink.

Without question, the *lei* made from *lehua*, the beautiful flowers of the *'ōhi'a* tree, is the most important legacy of *nā lei makamae*. Still readily available, the bright red color form (*lehua 'ula*) is the favorite color among the many chosen by contemporary *lei* makers.[41] Colors range from dark red (*lehua 'āpane*), red, and pink/coral to peach, pale yellow (*lehua melemele*) and strong yellow (*lehua mamo*), to orange (*lehua 'alani*) and gold. A white form (*lehua pua kea*) is rare. Altogether, there are some eighteen descriptive terms and synonyms for the various flower color variations.

Top: *Ulunuiokamamalu Garmon and Kekuhi Kanahele,*
  Kīlauea, Hawai'i
Right: *Kana'i Tegman, Pu'ukapu, Hawai'i*
Left: **Lei lehua 'ula**

A *lei* of red *lehua* is sacred to both Pele
and Hi'iaka; forests of the trees in Puna were
Hi'iaka's own sacred groves.[19] The red *lei
lehua* is mentioned more than a dozen times
in Emerson's *Myth of Pele and Hi'iaka* and, at
least once, suggests sexual arousal. Near the
end of the myth, Hi'iaka sits alone with
Lohi'au at the edge of Kīlauea Crater in Pele's
presence. Lohi'au, the handsome young chief
brought from Kaua'i by Hi'iaka for Pele's
pleasure, is the object of the following: "For
Hi'iaka, having gathered a lapful of that
passion-bloom, the scarlet *lehua,* and having
plaited three wreaths . . . hangs two of the
wreaths about the neck of Lohi'au, using the
third for her own adornment." Quickly, and,
apparently without objection, Lohi'au is
aroused by Hi'iaka's advances and happily
succumbs to her wiles.[19]

115

ʻŌhiʻa

Metrosideros polymorpha

Mai ka moku lehua ʻula
Ā i Lehua o ka moku kāʻili lā
ʻO ke alaloa hoʻi a ka lā
He ʻikena kūliʻu o ka hōpoe lehua lā!

From the land of the red *lehua*
To the sun-snatching island of Lehua
It is the long pathway of the sun
A profound image of the full-bloom *lehua.*
—P. K. K.

Bottom: Kekuhi Kanahele,
Keauhou, Kaʻū, Hawaiʻi
Right: ʻOʻilipua Kaikaina, Lehua Hauaniu, Nalani
Kanakaʻole, Pualani Kanahele, and Hokulani Kaikaina,
Kīlauea, Hawaiʻi

Left: **Lei liko lehua** *with* **palai**
Center: **Lei lehua ʻalani**
Right: **Lei lehua melemele**

'Ōhi'a
Metrosideros polymorpha

'Ōhi'a 'Ai
Syzygium malaccense

A relative of the *'ōhi'a* tree, *'ōhi'a 'ai*, or mountain apple, is a large tree that may attain heights of 75 feet, bearing masses of flowers similar in size and shape to those of *'ōhi'a*. The flowers may be deep pink, light pink, or, rarely, white, and are followed by edible fruit, also varying in color from red and various pinks to white. Both blossom and fruit are used to make *lei*[25] and were among the plant offerings placed on the *kuahu hula*.[18]

'Ōhi'a 'ai is another Polynesian introduction. It grows quickly and has become naturalized on the main Islands, where groves of *'ōhi'a 'ai* may be found in moist ravines. From times past, it has been cultivated.

Left: Kaliko Kaiwi,
Waimea, Hawai'i
Center: Kainoa Hodson,
Waimea, Hawai'i
*Right: Kai Espere, lei with **kupukupu**,*
Kalāhuipua'a, Hawai'i

'Ai 'ia ka hua
Wilia ka pua
'O ka 'ōhi'a 'ai o uka

The fruit is eaten
The flower woven
It is the upland *'ōhi'a 'ai*
—P. K. K.

'Ōlapa
Cheirodendron trigynum

The *'ōlapa* pictured is one of five endemic species. A small to medium tree, it grows from 15 to 45 feet tall in mid-elevation wet forests on all the main Islands except Kaho'olawe.

'Ōlapa leaves move in the slightest breeze with an interesting, vacillating motion. This quality has given rise to the naming of one of the two basic types of *hula*. 'Ōlapa dances are usually performed by young dancers, whose quick movements bring to mind the image of *'ōlapa* foliage flashing in the wind. Older dancers perform *hula ho'opa'a*, less vigorous, more sedate dances, sometimes seated.

We have no early written documentation to verify including *lei 'ōlapa* among *nā lei makamae*. However, a highly reputable contemporary source, Kepā Maly, notes its use in *lei*, and there is ample tradition of its being used by *lei* makers and dancers. In the mid-1970s, *kūpuna* attending a *hula* performance in Hilo observed dancers wearing *lei 'ōlapa* and remarked with pleasure and excitement that it had been many years since they had seen the wearing of this special *lei*.[49]

Kawaiponimō'ī Correa, Ni'eni'e, Hawai'i

122

E hīpuʻu i ka ʻōlapa
E hoʻolei i ka ʻōlapa
Ā e ʻōlapa pū ana lāua

Tie together the ʻōlapa leaves
Put the lei on the dancer
And together they will dance
—P. K. K.

123

'Ōlulu
Brighamia insignis

'Ōlulu is an extremely rare and endan-gered species endemic to sea cliffs from just above the reach of waves to 1,200 feet elevation on Ni'ihau and Kaua'i. It may grow from 3 feet to as much as 15 feet high, a succulent unbranched plant bearing sweetly scented, whitish yellow flowers. The combination of fragrance and yellowish color is irresistible to the *lei* maker. (See also *pua 'ala*, p. 138. The two species of *Brighamia* have been split from Rock's original *Brighamia insignis*.)

   Note: Flowers used in making the *lei* pictured were collected entirely from cultivated plants.

No Kaua'i mai 'o ka 'ōlulu,
Ka pua 'ena nohopali,
E ka 'ōlulu, hiki anei ke honi
I ka pua ke'oke'o ou?
'O kou nani paha
No ka 'ohu ka'a wale.

A demure cliff dweller
'Ōlulu is from Kaua'i
Say, *'ōlulu*, is it possible to inhale
That white flower of yours?
Perhaps your beauty
Is only for the passing cloud.
—*P. K. K.*

Mi Nei and Leiola Oliver, **lei** *with* **palai,** *Puhi, Kaua'i*

Pa'iniu

Astelia menziesiana

P *a'iniu* is found on all the main Islands except Ni'ihau and Kaho'olawe, from elevations of 1,800 feet to fairly high altitudes, up to 6,600 feet. Variable in habitat, it grows in bogs, rain forest, and semi-dry areas. It can be seen as an epiphyte growing in large colonies in crotches of trees or growing on the ground in highly organic soil or in cinder.

The startling silver foliage is collected and fashioned into a *lei*. In the early days, visitors to Kīlauea Volcano wore hat *lei* made of *pa'iniu* leaves, sometimes mixed with other foliage or flowers, to show that they had made the journey to Kīlauea Crater.[54]

'Ōliliko ka lauhina kilika
Wilia me ka lehua 'ula
He lei pono ia no ke akua

The silver silk leaf shimmers
Accented with the red *lehua*
An adornment fit for the god
—*P. K. K.*

*Kahealani Bertelmann, **lei** with **liko lehua**, and Pa'ula'ula Hauanio, Kīpuka 'Āinahou, Hawai'i*

Pala

Marattia douglasii

Once plentiful, the endemic fern *pala* is now rare. It thrives in high-rainfall areas at low to middle elevations. A large fern, *pala* stipes (stems) may be 5 feet long. Hawaiians relished baked *pala* stipe bases, made a pleasant drink from its leaf bases, and employed the plant for medicinal uses.[31] Feral pigs have taken their toll, as they eat its succulent fronds and short trunk.

Pala in traditional Hawai'i had many ceremonial uses. It was the symbol of Kāne, the god of life, and was used to decorate the short god (*akua poko*) of the Makahiki on the day of Kāne. Short *lei* of *pala* were fastened to the top horizontal pole of the Makahiki idol.[48] Pieces of *pala* were added to a *lei maile* to enhance its fragrance.[30]

Nalani Kanaka'ole, lei with maile, Waiākea, Hawai'i

128

Kupukupu a mōhala i luna
Ka pala lau a ka wahine
I pā'ū e kākua 'ia
I lewa pau a ka 'oni kīkala
E 'ami 'oi ola honua!

Sprouting full upward
Pala fern choice of the woman
To a skirt to be secured
To hips flying in motion
Dance while there is still yet time!
—*P. K. K.*

Lama log with yellow kapa, *symbol of*
***Laka with* lei pala *and* lei lehua**

Pala'ā

Odontosoria chinensis

An indigenous fern, *pala'ā* is also found in many other areas of the tropical Pacific. Usually seen as a delicate, clumping ground cover about 30 inches high, fronds may grow to 5 feet in ideal conditions. *Pala'ā* is a relatively common fern found in moist habitats at elevations from near sea level to 4,000 feet on all the main Islands except Kaho'olawe and Ni'ihau.

One of Pele's attendants, and Hi'iaka's faithful companion during the early stages of her mythical journey to Kaua'i, was *Pā'ū-o-Pala'ā,* meaning "the skirt of *pala'ā* fern."[19] *Pala'ā* was sacred to Hi'iaka.

Lei makers gather *pala'ā* to make a beautiful, soft *lei* or to add its fine-textured fronds to other *lei* materials. As a binding braid for a *lei haku,* its delicacy provides a comfortable base to protect the bare skin of the wearer.

E pala'ā, 'o Hi'iaka-i-ka-'iu-o-ka-moku
Ke kinolau kāhiko kaulana no nā 'ōlapa
Ā la'a no ke akua

O *pala'ā,* you are Hi'iaka-the-sacred-of-the-island
The exalted adornment of the dancers
A venerated symbol for the god
—*P. K. K.*

Lahela Chandler, Kē'ē, Kaua'i

130

Palai

Microlepia strigosa

Native to Hawaiʻi, *palai* is also found on many other tropical Pacific Islands. Under ideal conditions, in moist areas at elevations between 750 and 6,000 feet, *palai* fronds may attain lengths of 5 feet or more.

In South Hawaiʻi, *palai* was one of the important plants placed on the *kuahu hula*[4] and dedicated to Laka, goddess of *hula*.[18] *Palai* is highly regarded by *lei* makers. Frequently preferred over other *lei* materials for its fragrance and suppleness, it may be used to make a *lei* by itself.[32] It is commonly added to other *lei* materials to provide a fine texture, which acts as a foil to heavier materials, and to provide a soft base to protect the bare skin of the wearer. *Palai* is another plant readily available for *lei mākamae*.

Palai

Microlepia strigosa

***Kimo Lim** with **lei maile**, Kalōpā, Hawai'i*
***Right:** **Lei palai** with **lei maile** on drum*

Mai palai aku, e ka palapalai
'O 'oe 'o Laka, ke kumu hula
'O 'oe ka lei, hilia me ke aloha
Ua kuahu 'ia me ka 'ōlapa
He kuahu no Laka

Do not turn self-consciously
You are Laka, the benevolent conscience of *hula*
You are the *lei*, woven with love
Placed on the dancer
An altar for Laka.   —*P. K. K.*

Pōhuehue

Ipomoea pes-caprae subsp. *brasiliensis*

Growing just above the reach of ocean waves, *pōhuehue,* or beach morning glory, forms a dense ground cover, protecting dunes from strong, erosive winds. Pantropical, *pōhuehue* is common throughout Hawai'i.

    Pōhuehue is traditionally associated with bewitching. Surfers, to summon better waves, whipped the sea with strands *(lei)* of *pōhuehue* while chanting the following:[27]

*Keoki Kalipi and Healani Kaholowa'a,
Ka'ili'ula, Moloka'i*

*Ku mai! Ku mai!
Ka nalu nui mai Kahiki mai
'Alo po'i pū
Kū mai i ka pōhuehue
Hū! Kaiko'o loa!*

Arise! Arise!
Great surfs from Kahiki
Waves break together!
Rise with the *pōhuehue*
Well up, raging surf!

Pōhuehue

Ipomoea pes-caprae subsp. *brasiliensis*

A person on shore sighting someone in a canoe whom he wished to kill would similarly whip the ocean with strands of *pōhuehue*, hoping to create dangerous waves that would overturn the canoe and drown his victim. Also, fishermen slapped the water with strands of *pōhuehue* to drive fish into nets. Nursing mothers sometimes substituted *pōhuehue* for *'uala* to increase the flow of milk.[27] (See also reference 30.)

'O ka pōhuehue kai holo
Holo i uka, holo i kai
No ke aha kona holo
I 'ō a i 'ane'i?
No ka wela o ke one

Pōhuehue runs upland
And seaward
Why does it run
Here and there?
Because the sand is so hot.
—P. K. K.

Keoki Kalipi and
Healani Kaholowa'a,
Ka'ili'ula, Moloka'i

Po'olā Nui

Bidens cosmoides

Found on Kaua'i in moderately moist forests at elevations between 2,000 and 3,000, *po'olā nui* bears large, pendant yellow flowers most of the year. It is one of twenty-two endemic *ko'oko'olau* (*Bidens* spp.). Hawaiians gave this *ko'oko'olau* a special name, indicating familiarity and a particular importance. Because other *ko'oko'olau* are used by *lei* makers on other Islands, we are confident that *po'olā nui* was similarly employed.

'O ka po'olā nui kau po'ohiwi
O ke po'o ho'olewa
'Oi aku kou nani
O nā pua melemele

Po'olā nui sits on the shoulder
Of the sacred chiefess
You are indeed more beautiful
Than all other yellow blossoms
—*P. K. K.*

Opposite page:
Kepola Flores, lei *with* palai, lei hulu,
Holoholokū, Kaua'i

Pua 'Ala
Brighamia rockii

Mapuana Makaiwi lei with palai, Kalawao, Kalaupapa, Moloka'i

An endangered and extremely rare endemic plant, *pua ʻala* is found on sea cliffs on windward Molokaʻi from just above the reach of ocean waves to 1,200 feet in elevation. It is a succulent, single-stemmed shrub reaching as much as 15 feet high. Strong trade winds and salt air almost constantly buffet the plants. In former times, Hawaiians in Wailau Valley cultivated *pua ʻala* around their homes. The pale yellow flowers are described as "sweet scented with an odor like that of violets."[56] The combination of yellow flowers and heady scent would make them eagerly sought by the *lei* maker.
(See also *ʻōlulu*, p. 124.)

Note: Flowers used in making the *lei* pictured were collected entirely from cultivated plants.

Moani ke ʻala o ka pua ʻala
I ka pō o Mōhalu
Huli ka manaʻo i ka pali loloa o Pelekunu
ʻAʻahu i ke kapa melemele, noho kuʻu puāhilo nō
Kuʻu pua ʻala

On the night of the *Mōhalu* moon
The scent of *pua ʻala* fills the air
Memory returns to the high cliffs of Pelekunu
Clothed in yellow *kapa*, sits my delicate flower
My *pua ʻala*
—*P. K. K.*

Pūkiawe
Styphelia tameiameiae

Pūkiawe is an indigenous shrub found in windward coastal sites. It is rare near sea level but common at high elevations to 9,000 feet on all the Islands except Ni'ihau and Kaho'olawe. *Pūkiawe* also grows in the Marquesas Islands. Highly variable, it may appear in treelike form or as an erect or spreading, dense shrub 9 or so feet tall, less at high elevations. The *lei* maker uses its white *liko* and small, spherical fruit, which may vary in color from white to pink to red.[30] (See also reference 1.)

Pūkiawe, pukuku'i 'elo'elo
Pūkiawe, puku'i i ke kēhau
Pūkiawe, kano i ka noe
Ka noe a Lilinoe
O ka 'iu o lono

Pūkiawe embraces the damp cold
Pūkiawe collects the dew
Pūkiawe, woody in the fine rain
The mist of Lilinoe
Who dwells in the summit
—P. K. K.

Puahone Foster and Kahana Pukahi, Waiākea, Hawaiʻi

'Uala
Ipomoea batatas

A major Hawaiian food source, *'uala* (sweet potato) is another Polynesian introduction from the south. Although now widely cultivated throughout the Tropics, it originated in tropical America in prehistoric times. It is a vine that roots at nodes and produces tubers of outstanding nutritional value. *'Uala* is capable of growing under a wide range of environmental conditions. Early Hawaiians grew more than two hundred different cultivars of *'uala*, most of which have disappeared.[68] Young leaves and stem tips, as well as the tubers, were relished.

Mōhala i ka hani a ka lā
Ka poni a ka pua 'uala
He pua nehenehe wale i kahi pu'epu'e
Na ke kā 'uala kēia mau nani e lawe

Blooming with the gentle persuasion of the sun
Are the purple blossoms of the sweet potato
A flower that creeps upon the contour of
    mounds
It is the vine that transports these beauties
—*P. K. K.*

For the *lei* maker, it is the milky sap of the vine that is of particular interest. A nursing mother, to increase the flow of milk, carried a bowl of springwater to the *'uala* field at dawn. There, while praying to Kū, she picked a length of vine with her right hand. Then she picked a second length of vine with her left hand while praying to Hina. She dipped the vine pieces into the springwater, gently slapping the right breast with the vine picked by her right hand and the left breast with the vine picked by her left hand. She wore the vines, tied together as a *lei,* around her neck for several days. This process of bruising the tender *'uala* vine released its symbolic white, milky sap, assuring the flow of mother's milk.[27] *Pōhuehue* vines could be substituted for *'uala*.[30] A *lei* made of another plant, *wauke mālolo (Broussonetia papyrifera)* (not pictured), was also employed to assure or increase the flow of milk.[28] This is the simple prayer directed to Kū and Hina:[27]

Ia ola 'e Kū me Hina
Ho mai ka waiu a nui a lawe a helehele'i
'Oia ka 'olua e ha'awi mai ai ka 'olua pula pula

That life O Kū and Hina
Extend [give] the milk till there is much and
     sufficient and scattered about.
That is for you to give to your offspring to
     multiply.

Luana Heinecki and son Kaimana, 'Anaeho'omalu, Hawai'i   143

Hooheno Sakamoto, Waimea, Hawai'i

Uhiuhi
Caesalpinia kavaiensis

Now rare and endangered, *uhiuhi* is a large shrub or small tree that may grow to 35 feet tall. At one time, *uhiuhi* grew sparingly from near sea level to elevations around 3,000 feet on Kaua'i, O'ahu, West Maui, and in the North Kona District on Hawai'i. *Uhiuhi* wood, hard and durable, was used by early Hawaiians for making spears and fishing implements.[54] Hawaiians were intimately aware of all the properties of this handsome tree. It produces highly attractive rose-colored flowers with a red margin, which are carefully collected by the *lei* maker.

The following chant excerpt describes the flowering of *uhiuhi* and *ko'oko'olau*. From the myth of Pele and Hi'iaka, it is a supplication to the gods protecting Hi'iaka during her successful battles with the Mahiki dragon and the great dragon Mo'olau[19] ("*ko'olau*" is an abbreviated form of "*ko'oko'olau*").[54]

A Mo'olau, i ka pua o ka uhiuhi
Helele'i mai ana ka pua ko'oko'olau.

In the wilds of Mo'olau
The *uhiuhi*'s time for bloom
The petals fall of *ko'olau*'s flower.

Note: Flowers used in making the *lei* pictured were gathered from a cultivated plant.

'O ka uhiuhi ka lā'au i hōlua mai lā
'O ka uhiuhi ka lā'au i ihe mai lā
'O ka uhiuhi ka lā'au i 'ō'ō mai lā
'O ka uhiuhi ka lā'au i pou hale mai lā
'O ka uhiuhi ka pua, ua pa'a ku'u lei

The *uhiuhi* wood becomes a sled
The *uhiuhi* wood becomes a spear
The *uhiuhi* wood becomes a digging tool
The *uhiuhi* wood becomes a house post
The flower is *uhiuhi*, my *lei* is complete

—P. K. K.

145

'Uki'uki
Dianella sandwicensis

Found on all the main Islands except Kaho'olawe and Ni'ihau, *'uki'uki,* which grows 2 to 3 feet tall, is a clumping member of the lily family producing bright blue to dark blue fruit used to make a striking *lei.*[8] The fruit is also used to produce a smoky blue *kapa* dye.[10] *'Uki'uki* grows in a wide variety of environments at elevations between 300 and 6,000 feet, from semi-dry, wet, and lightly shaded areas to locations in full sun. Contemporary *kapa* makers have speculated that *'uki'uki* fruit, which is juicy, when strung into *lei* would be protected from pressure that would result from being packed in containers. In *lei* form, the fruits would retain their useful juice during transport.

He aha kēia mea kanu?
*   He mau oho uliuli,*
*   Waiho'olu'u o ke kai hohonu*
*   Lilia pouli!*
He mea kanu 'uki'uki me ka hua uliuli.

What is this plant?
    Strands of blue,
    Coloring of the deep sea,
    Dark lily
An *'uki'uki* plant with the dark fruit. —*P. K. K.*

Kainoa Hodson, Pu'ukapu, Hawai'i

146

'Ūlei
Osteomeles anthyllidifolia

'Ūlei grows at elevations ranging from sea level to above 6,000 feet, in a wide range of habitats: salty, windswept coastal sites, dry to semi-wet areas, and sunny to lightly shaded places. In harsh environments, it may be seen as a low, ground-hugging shrub 2 to 3 feet tall, but in areas with more suitable climates, it may take on a slender, almost treelike shape 9 to 15 feet tall. 'Ūlei grows on all the main Islands except Kaho'olawe and Ni'ihau. It is indigenous and also is found in the Cook Islands and Tonga.

The leaves have medicinal applications. In times past, the long, pliant stems were used as frames for fishnets, and the strong, dense wood was fashioned into digging sticks and fish spears. The *lei* maker seeking *'ūlei* will gather both the small, clustered white fruit and the white flowers.[1]

Mōhala ka pua 'ūlei
I ka 'ao'ao kona o Ka'ū
Kahi a po'e lawai'a
Ho'omākaukau i ka lā'au 'ūlei
No ka 'upena uluulu
I nā wāhine ke wili pua nei
I mau oho e kau ma ka lauoho

'Ūlei blooms
On the leeward of Ka'ū
There, where the fishermen
Prepare the supple branches
For the large scoop nets,
While women plait the flowers
Into strands to nestle in their hair.
—*P. K. K.*

Maile Kealoha, **lei** *with* 'a'ali'i *and* **palai***, Waimea, Hawai'i*

Wāwae'iole

Lycopodium cernuum

Wāwae'iole literally means "rat foot," perhaps referring to the scaly surface of the plant or to the clawlike character of its foliage. It is found throughout the Tropics in wet areas and in Hawai'i from near sea level to 4,500 feet elevation.

The tough, long-lasting branch tips were used to make *lei*, frequently as a background for other, more colorful material or mixed with ferns.[45] *Wāwae'iole* is a clubmoss; Isabela Bird describes *lei* made with "mosses."[8] The plants may reach heights of 5 feet. A somewhat related spikemoss, *lepelepeamoa* (not pictured), was also used with more colorful materials to fashion *lei*.[54]

Mā'aweawe ke ki'i palanehe
A ka wāwae'iole nahele
'A'ohe wahi koe a ka 'iole
Ahuwale nā mēheu heluhelu
Helua a māne'one'o ka lae kanaka

Faint are the delicate steps
In a stand of *wāwae'iole*
No one escapes the traces of this plant
Plain to the eyes the scratchy tracks
Tickle the forehead of man.   —*P. K. K.*

Ulumauahi Santiago, **lei po'o** *with*
pūkiawe, lehua, palai, *and* **kupukupu,**
Pi'opi'o, Hawai'i   149

Wiliwili

Erythrina sandwicensis

Endemic trees, *wiliwili* are found growing both singly and in groves in dry areas from near sea level to about 1,800 feet elevation on all the main Islands. They may reach heights of 50 feet. All parts of the tree are useful. In particular, the light-weight wood is ideal for fashioning surfboards, fishnet floats, and out-riggers for canoes. The flowers[19] and seeds,[20] sought by the *lei* maker, vary in color from red orange to orange, yellow to chartreuse, and, rarely, white. Some flowers display two colors. Seed color is also variable, from dark red to light red, orange, and pale yellow.[57]

Wiliwili wilia nā lau e ke ahe
Nā lau holuholu napenape
A helelei, helelei a helele'i
He 'ano'ano kekē 'ula i ka lā
Kekē ka pae niho wakawaka
Wāwena ka mākau a ke aloha

The *wiliwili* quakes in the breeze
The leaves rising and falling
Scattered, scattered below
Seeds exposing red in the sun
Exposed stand the rows of serrated teeth
Hot is the skill of the lover.   —*P. K. K.*

Wiliwili
Erythrina sandwicensis

Above: Maliaokalani Ahana and Lunamaka'āinana Pascual, Lālāmilo, Hawai'i
Left: Hanalei Fergerstrom, lei hua, Kawaihae, Hawai'i

The light-weight wood of *wiliwili* was used in early Hawai'i for fashioning *lei palaoa wiliwili*,[20] a carved, hook-shaped pendant secured about the neck by braided human hair. The more elegant *lei niho palaoa*, made of whale or seal ivory, was a symbol of royalty.[15] Early forms of this singular *lei* were made of wood, shell, or bone or whale ivory.[44] Later, after contact with whalers, whale and walrus ivory became more readily available.

Peneku Kaʻae with **lei palaoa wiliwili,** *Keaukaha, Hawaiʻi*

Wiliwili
Erythrina sandwicensis

An interesting account involving *wiliwili* tells of King ʻUmi-a-Līloa of Waipiʻo, who visited Hilo incognito. He was young and handsome and not long after his arrival married the daughter of the King of Hilo. One evening, during a "grand entertainment," he became upset seeing his new wife wearing a *lei palaoa wiliwili,* a pendant carved from *wiliwili* wood rather than one fashioned from the chiefly whale ivory in accordance with the couple's *aliʻi* status. In a fit of pique, ʻUmi destroyed his wife's *lei palaoa wiliwili,* thereby offending the King of Hilo. His rash act began a string of battles that eventually resulted in ʻUmi's dominance over the entire Island of Hawaiʻi.[20]

"Although many of the techniques used for making lei
are documented in historical resource material,
the structure of a lei *may also*
be determined by the lei *maker.*
It is part of the creativity
involved in this particular art form.
Experienced lei *makers know from*
the size, shape, and texture of the lei *material*
which technique or techniques may best be employed.
This knowledge has been passed down
from one generation to the next,
in much the same way as have
the movements, sounds, and tempos of the hula,
or the vocal character of a chant.
These are ephemeral arts:
once a hula *has been performed,*
its movements and sounds are gone.
So it is with the short-lived beauty of the lei."

APPENDIX A

Lei Plant Names and Synonyms

VOCABULARY OF PLANT PARTS USED IN MAKING LEI

---

hua	fruit, seed	*limu*	water plants, mosses, lichens
hue	gourd	*mu'o*	leaf bud
'ili	bark	*nu'a*	thick, white young leaves
lā'au	plant	*'ōpu'u*	bud
lau	leaf	*pua*	flower
liko	newly opened colored leaf		

HAWAIIAN NAME	PLANT PART USED	SCIENTIFIC NAME AND FAMILY
'a'ali'i syn. *'a'ali'i kū makani,* *'a'ali'i kū ma kua, kūmakani*	*hua, lau*	*Dodonaea viscosa* Sapindaceae (Soapberry Family)
a'e syn. *mānele*	*hua*	*Sapindus saponaria* Sapindaceae (Soapberry Family)
a'e syn. *hea'e, kāwa'u,* *kawau kua kuku kapa, mānele*	*hua*	*Zanthoxylum dipetalum* Rutaceae (Rue Family)
'ahu'awa syn. *'ehu'awa*	*pua*	*Mariscus javanicus* Cyperaceae (Sedge Family)
'aiakanēnē syn. *kūkaenēnē, leponēnē,* *nēnē, pūnēnē*	*hua*	*Coprosma ernodeoides* Rubiaceae (Coffee Family)
'ākia syn. *'ākia lau nui, 'ākia* *mānalo, 'ākia pehu, kauhi*	*pua, hua, lau*	*Wikstroemia pulcherrima* Thymelaeaceae ('Ākia Family)
'ākōlea	*lau*	*Athyrium microphyllum* Athyriaceae (Lady Fern Family)
'ākulikuli 'ae'ae syn. *'ae'ae, 'ākulikuli kai,* *'ākulikuli 'ōhelo, 'ōhelo kai*	*hua*	*Lycium sandwicense* Solanaceae (Nightshade Family)

HAWAIIAN NAME	PLANT PART USED	SCIENTIFIC NAME AND FAMILY
alahe'e syn. *'ōhe'a, walahe'e*	*pua, lau*	*Canthium odoratum* Rubiaceae (Coffee Family)
alani syn. *alani kuahiwi*	*hua, lau*	*Melicope oahuensis* Rutaceae (Rue Family)
'awapuhi syn. *'awapuhi kuahiwi, 'ōpuhi*	*lau*	*Zingiber zerumbet* Zingiberaceae (Ginger Family)
'āwikiwiki syn. *puakauhi*	*pua*	*Canavalia galeata* and *C. hawaiiensis* Fabaceae (Bean Family)
hala syn. *lauala, lauhala, pū hala* (See p. 17 for fruit color variations: *hala 'īkoi, hala lihilihi 'ula, hala melemele, hala pia* and *hala 'ula*.)	*hua*	*Pandanus tectorius* Pandanaceae (Screwpine Family)
hala pepe syn. *le'ie*	*pua*	*Pleomele hawaiiensis* Agavaceae (Agave Family)
hau syn. *hau ka'eka'e* *hau ko'i'i, hau oheohe*	*pua, 'ili*	*Hibiscus tiliaceus* Malvaceae (Hibiscus Family)
hinahina kū kahakai syn. *hinahina, nohonoho,* *pu'uone* (Ni'ihau), *pōhinahina*	*pua, lau*	*Heliotropium anomalum* var. *argenteum* Boraginaceae (Borage Family)
hīnano	*pua, lau*	*Pandanus tectorius* Pandanaceae (Screwpine Family)
'ie'ie syn. *'ie*	*lau*	*Freycinetia arborea* Pandanaceae (Screwpine Family)
'iliahi syn. *'a'ahi, 'ala, 'aoa* *lā'au 'ala, wahie 'ala*	*pua, lau*	*Santalum haleakalae* Santalaceae (Sandalwood Family)
'iliahialo'e syn. *'a'ahi, 'ala, 'aoa, 'iliahi,* *lā'au, lā'au 'ala, wahie 'ala*	*pua, lau*	*Santalum ellipticum* Santalaceae (Sandalwood Family)

HAWAIIAN NAME	PLANT PART USED	SCIENTIFIC NAME AND FAMILY
'ilima syn. *'ilima koli kukui, 'ilima kuahiwi, 'ilima kū kahakai, 'ilima kū kula, 'ilima lei, 'ilima makana'ā, 'ilima mamo, 'ilima ōkea, 'ilima papa, kolikukui.*	*pua*	*Sida fallax* Malvaceae (Hibiscus Family)
ipu syn. *hue, ipu nui, pōhue*	*hue*	*Lagenaria siceraria* Cucurbitaceae (Gourd Family)
kāmakahala	*pua*	*Labordia degeneri* Loganiaceae (Strychnine Family)
kamani syn. *kamanu, tamanu*	*pua*	*Calophyllum inophyllum* Clusiaceae (Mangosteen Family)
kauna'oa syn. *kauna'oa lei, kauna'oa kahakai, kauno'a* (Ni'ihau), *pōlolo*	*lā'au*	*Cuscuta sandwichiana* Cuscutaceae (Dodder Family)
kī syn. *'āpi'i, ti*	*lau*	*Cordyline fruticosa* Agavaceae (Agave Family)
kō	*pua*	*Saccharum officinarum* Poaceae (Grass Family)
koa	*lau*	*Acacia koa* Fabaceae (Bean Family)
koai'a syn. *koai'e, koa 'ohā*	*pua, lau*	*Acacia koaia (A. koa)* Fabaceae (Bean Family)
koali syn. *koali 'ai, koali 'ai'ai* (Ni'ihau), *koali lau manamana, pa'ali'i*	*lau*	*Ipomoea cairica* Convolvulaceae (Morning Glory Family)
koki'o syn. *hau hele 'ula*	*pua*	*Kokia drynarioides* Malvaceae (Hibiscus Family)
koki'o ke'oke'o syn. *koki'o kea, pāmakani*	*pua*	*Hibiscus arnottianus* subsp. *punaluuensis* Malvaceae (Hibiscus Family)
koki'o syn. *koki'o 'ula, koki'o 'ula'ula, mākū, pualoalo*	*pua*	*Hibiscus kokia* Malvaceae (Hibiscus Family)

HAWAIIAN NAME	PLANT PART USED	SCIENTIFIC NAME AND FAMILY
kōlea lau liʻi syn. *kōlea*	*liko*	*Myrsine sandwicensis* Myrsinaceae (Myrsine Family)

kolokolo kahakai
  syn. *hinahina kolo, mānawanawa,*
  mānewanewa, māwanawana,
  pōhinahina, pōlinalina (Oʻahu)
	pua, lau	*Vitex rotundifolia*
		Verbenaceae (Verbena Family)

koʻokoʻolau
  syn. *kokolau, kōkoʻolau, koʻokolau,*
  koʻolau
	pua	*Bidens menziesii* subsp. *filiformis*
		Asteraceae (Sunflower Family)

koʻoloaʻula	*pua*	*Abutilon menziesii* Malvaceae (Hibiscus Family)
kou	*pua*	*Cordia subcordata* Boraginaceae (Borage Family)
kukui syn. *kuikui*	*pua, hua, lau*	*Aleurites moluccana* Euphorbiaceae (Euphorbia Family)

kupaliʻi
  syn. *ʻalaʻala wai nui, ʻalaʻala wai*
  nui pua kī, ʻalaʻala wai nui wahine
	lau	*Plectranthus parviflorus*
		Lamiaceae (Mint Family)

kūpaoa
  syn. *hanupaoa, hinaʻaikamalama,*
  kupaua, naʻenaʻe, neʻineʻi
	pua, lau	*Dubautia scabra*
		Asteraceae (Sunflower Family)

kupukupu
  syn. *niʻaniʻau, ʻōkupukupu,*
  palapalai (Niʻihau), *pāmoho*
	lau	*Nephrolepis exaltata* and *N. cordifolia*
		Nephrolepidiaceae (Sword Fern Family)

lauaʻe syn. *peʻahi*	*lau*	*Microsorum spectrum* Polypodiaceae (Polypody Fern Family)

lehua ʻāhihi
  syn. *ʻāhihi, ʻāhihi kū ma kua,*
  ʻāhihi lehua, kūmakua, ʻōhiʻa ʻāhihi
	pua	*Metrosideros tremuloides*
		Myrtaceae (Eucalyptus Family)

lepelepeamoa		*Selaginella arbuscula* Selaginaceae (Spikemoss Family)
limu kala syn. *kala*	*limu*	*Sargassum echinocarpum* Sargassaceae (Sargassum Family)

160

HAWAIIAN NAME	PLANT PART USED	SCIENTIFIC NAME AND FAMILY
limu pāhapaha syn. *pāhapaha* (Kaua'i), *pāhapaha-o-Polihale, pakaia* (Hawai'i), *pālahalaha, pāpahapaha* (Kaua'i and O'ahu)	*limu*	*Ulva fasciata* Ulvaceae (Ulva Family)
mai'a	*lau*	*Musa* x *paradisiaca* Musaceae (Banana Family)
maile syn. *maile ha'i wale, maile kaluhea,* *maile lau li'i, maile lau li'ili'i, maile* *lau nui, maile pākaha* (See p. 84 for pictured leaf variations.)	*lau*	*Alyxia oliviformis* Apocynaceae (Dogbane Family)
māmane syn. *mamani*	*pua*	*Sophora chrysophylla* Fabaceae (Bean Family)
mānewanewa syn. *kolokolo kahakai*	*pua, lau*	*Vitex rotundifolia* Verbenaceae (Verbena Family)
manono	*lau*	*Hedyotis centranthoides* Rubiaceae (Coffee Family)
ma'o syn. *huluhulu*	*pua*	*Gossypium tomentosum* Malvaceae (Hibiscus Family)
milo	*pua*	*Thespesia populnea* Malvaceae (Hibiscus Family)
moa syn. *moa nahele, 'o'omoa, pipi*	*lā'au*	*Psilotum nudum* Psilotaceae (Whisk-Fern Family)
mokihana syn. *alani, alani kuahiwi*	*hua*	*Melicope anisata* Rutaceae (Rue Family)
na'ena'e syn. *hanupaoa, hina-'ai-ka-malama,* *kūpaoa, kupaua, ne'ine'i*	*pua, lau*	*Dubautia ciliolata* subsp. *ciliolata* Asteraceae (Sunflower Family)
nānū syn. *nā'ū*	*pua*	*Gardenia brighamii* Rubiaceae (Coffee Family)
naupaka kahakai syn. *aupaka* (Kaua'i), *huahekili,* *naupaka, naupaka kai*	*pua, hua, lau*	*Scaevola sericea* Goodeniaceae (Naupaka Family)

HAWAIIAN NAME	PLANT PART USED	SCIENTIFIC NAME AND FAMILY
naupaka kuahiwi syn. *naupaka*	*pua*	*Scaevola gaudichaudiana* Goodeniaceae (Naupaka Family)
nehe	*pua, lau*	*Lipochaeta lavarum* Asteraceae (Sunflower Family)
neke syn. *palae, uiui*	*lau*	*Cyclosorus interruptus* Thelypteridaceae (Maiden Fern Family)
niu syn. ololani	*pua*	*Cocos nucifera* Arecaceae (Palm Family)
nohoanu syn. *hinahina*	*pua, lau*	*Geranium cuneatum* subsp. *hololeucum* Geraniaceae (Geranium Family)
nuku ʻiʻwi syn. *kāiʻiwi, kaiwi, nuku, nukuiwi*	*pua*	*Strongylodon ruber* Fabaceae (Bean Family)
ʻōhā syn. *hāhā, ʻōhā wai*	*pua*	*Clermontia kohalae* Campanulaceae (Bellflower Family)
ʻōhai	*pua*	*Sesbania tomentosa* Fabaceae (Bean Family)
ʻōhelo syn. *ʻōhelo ʻai*	*pua, hua, lau, liko*	*Vaccinium reticulatum* Ericaceae (Heath Family)
ʻōhiʻa syn. *lehua, ʻōhiʻa lehua*	*pua, liko, lau, hua,* *ʻōpuʻu, muʻo, nuʻa*	*Metrosideros polymorpha* Myrtaceae (Eucalyptus Family)
ʻōhiʻa ʻai syn. *ʻōhiʻa*	*pua, hua*	*Syzygium malaccense* Myrtaceae (Eucalyptus Family)
ʻōlapa syn. *ehu, kauila māhu* (Maui), *lapalapa, māhu, ʻōlapalapa*	*lau*	*Cheirodendron trigynum* Araliaceae (Aralia Family)
ʻōlulu syn. *ālula, hāhā, pua ʻala,* *pū aupaka*	*pua*	*Brighamia insignis* Campanulaceae (Bellflower Family)
paʻiniu syn. *kaluaha, puaʻakuhinia*	*lau*	*Astelia menziesiana* Liliaceae (Lily Family)
pala syn. *kapuaʻilio*	*lau*	*Marattia douglasii* Marattiaceae (Mulesfoot Fern Family)

HAWAIIAN NAME	PLANT PART USED	SCIENTIFIC NAME AND FAMILY
pala'ā syn. *pala'e, palapala'ā,* *pa'u o Pala'e*	*lau*	*Odontosoria chinensis* Lindsaeaceae (Lace Fern Family)
palai syn. *la'a, palai ali'i, palai 'ula,* *palapalae, palapalai*	*lau*	*Microlepia strigosa* Dennstaedtiaceae (Hay-Scented Fern Family)
pōhuehue syn. *puhuehue*	*lā'au*	*Ipomoea pes-caprae* subsp. *brasiliensis* Convolvulaceae (Morning Glory Family)
po'olā nui	*pua*	*Bidens cosmoides* Asteraceae (Sunflower Family)
pua 'ala syn. *ālula, hāhā, 'ōlulu, pū aupaka*	*pua*	*Brighamia rockii* Campanulaceae (Bellflower Family)
pūkiawe syn. *'a'ali'i mahu, kānehoa, mu'o,* *nu'a kāwa'u (Lāna'i, Maui),* *maiele, maieli, puakeawe, puakiawe,* *pukeawe, pūpūkiawe*	*hua, lau*	*Styphelia tameiameiae* Epacridaceae (Epacris Family)
'uala syn. *'uwala*	*lā'au*	*Ipomoea batatas* Convolvulaceae (Morning Glory Family)
uhiuhi syn. *kāwa'u (Maui), kea*	*pua*	*Caesalpinia kavaiensis* Fabaceae (Bean Family)
'uku'uki syn. *'uki*	*hua*	*Dianella sandwicensis* Liliaceae (Lily Family)
'ūlei syn. *eluehe (Moloka'i), 'u'ulei*	*pua, hua, lau, mu'o*	*Osteomeles anthyllidifolia* Rosaceae (Rose Family)
wauke mālolo syn. *po'a'aha, wauke*	*lau*	*Broussonetia papyrifera* Moraceae (Mulberry Family)
wāwae'iole syn. *hulu 'iole, huluhulu-a-'iole*	*lau*	*Lycopodium cernuum* Lycopodiaceae (Club Moss Family)
wiliwili	*pua, hua*	*Erythrina sandwicensis* Fabaceae (Bean Family)

*"Today, much of the native Hawaiian flora is threatened,
and many species are endangered.
We strongly urge anyone
who normally gathers* lei *material from the wild
to realize that many of the plants depicted in*
Nā Lei Makamae
*can be grown under cultivation,
thus removing pressure from wild populations.
Toward this end,
Appendix B provides a complete list of the* lei *plants,
simple directions for their propagation,
and sources of propagating material
other than from the wild."*

APPENDIX B
Lei Plant Propagation

We know that in early times in the Islands, Hawaiians cultivated at least five native plant species as a source of *lei* materials: *ʻilima, kokiʻo, kokiʻo ʻula, kokiʻo keʻo keʻo, nukuʻiʻiwi, pua ʻala,* and perhaps *ʻōlulu.* Other *lei* plants may have been plentiful and readily accessible, making the effort of cultivating them unnecessary. At least an equal number of Polynesian introductions, then under common cultivation, were also used by the *lei* maker: *ʻawapuhi, hala, hau, ipu, kamani, kī, kō, kou, kukui, maiʻa, ʻōhiʻa ʻai.* Both native and introduced plants had many other uses, but we are concerned here solely with their use in *nā lei makamae.* They were part of the immediate environment and were encountered daily.

Serious *lei* makers of today, especially those engaged in the *hālau hula,* are urged to propagate and cultivate their own *lei* materials. An examination of the lists of *nā lei makamae* plants listed below quickly reveals that almost three-quarters of them are adaptable to low-elevation growing. Forty-one of these are regularly available at botanical garden plant sales sponsored by their support groups: on Oʻahu, these are the Friends of Honolulu Botanical Gardens at Foster Garden and Hoʻomaluhia, and the Lyon Arboretum Association, and Waimea Arboretum Foundation; on Kauaʻi, Nā Lima Kōkua (National Tropical Botanical Garden); and on Hawaiʻi, the Amy Greenwell Ethnobotanical Garden. On Maui, contact the Maui Native Plant Society for referrals to reputable growers. Also, refer to the lists below. We strongly urge the *lei* maker to obtain established plants from the above sources, cultivate them, and then propagate from that stock. When at sales, talk with the vendors or garden staff. They have practical experience and are generous with valuable information. Species not normally found at sales may usually be ordered either from the garden involved or the vendors.

Stay out of the mountains and off the shorelines when obtaining propagating material. Indiscriminate but well-intentioned collecting from wild populations can be devastating to the gene pool. Please let the experts collect wisely for you. The unwise acquisition of any rare plant from the wild anywhere on our planet cannot be justified.

A word of caution about growing endangered native species: it is against federal and state law to collect plants, cuttings, or seed from any wild plant. This stricture pertains whether the plants are growing on private or public property. A permit to collect must be obtained from the Department of Land and Natural Resources, State of Hawaiʻi. Contact the U.S. Fish and Wildlife Service for further restrictions relating to federal lands. It is permissible, however, to purchase properly labeled endangered species from a licensed source, such as vendors at the regular garden plant sales noted above. Many *lei*-making species are available.

Our *lei makamae* list carries the following endangered species: *ʻākulikuli ʻaeʻae, hala pepe, kokiʻo, koʻoloaʻula, nānū, ʻōhai, ʻōlulu, pua ʻala,* and *uhiuhi.* It is sad to reflect on the fact that these species, once commonly found in the Islands, are now critically rare and must be protected by stringent laws. All are recommended for growing in lowland *lei* gardens.

To get a good start on your native plant *lei* garden, we urge a simple mental exercise: What is the environment of your growing space? Sunny, shaded, windy? What is the nature of your soil? The wide majority of native plants require excellent drainage; most require regular watering. Even dryland species will thrive if given regular moisture in open, well-drained soil. Select a few native plants requiring similar environments, and begin with those. Move slowly and intelligently. Avoid overplanting, which can lead to sick plants, weeds, and a frustrated grower. Remember to get information at plant sales from experienced gardeners before you make a final selection and begin planting. Your first home-grown *lei* will be exciting and rewarding.

Plants are propagated by several means. We are recommending only three methods for the amateur propagator: by cuttings, by seed, and by division. Requiring far more expertise, certain plants may also be propagated by grafting, air-layering, ground-layering, spores (ferns), and tissue culture.

The following lists should be helpful. Plants are grouped according to propagation method and sun-shade requirements.

A. Species from Seed for Planting Out in Full Sun

'a'ali'i
a'e (*Sapindus* spp.)
a'e (*Zanthoxylum* spp.)
'ākia
'ākulikuli 'ae 'ae (best along the coast)
alahe'e
alani
'āwikiwiki
hala
hala pepe
hau
hinahina kū kahakai (best along the coast)
'iliahi
'iliahialo'e (best along the coast)
'ilima

kamani
koa
koai'a
koki'o
koki'o ke'o ke'o
koki'o 'ula
kolokolo kahakai
ko'oko'olau
ko'oloa'ula
kou
kukui
kupali'i
lehua 'āhihi
māmane
mānewanewa
manono
ma'o
milo
nānū
naupaka kahakai (best along the coast)
naupaka kuahiwi
nehe
niu
nuku'i'iwi
'ōhai
'ōhi'a 'ai
'ōhi'a lehua (Seedlings may not "come true"; i.e., bear flowers and *liko* the same as on the parent plant.)
'ōlulu
pōhuehue
po'olā nui
pua 'ala
pūkiawe
uhiuhi
'uki'uki
'ūlei
wiliwili (Seedlings may not "come true" to parent flower color from seed.)

166

B. Species from Seed for Planting Out in Shade

'ie 'ie
kōlea lau li'i
maile
mokihana

C. Species from Cuttings for Planting Out in Sun

'ākia
'ākulikuli 'ae 'ae
'āwikiwiki
hau
hinihina kū kahakai (best along the coast)
'ilima
kī
kō
koali
koki'o ke'o ke'o
koki'o 'ula
kolokolo kahakai
ko'oko'olau
ko'oloa'ula
kupali'i
lehua 'āhihi
mānewanewa
manono
ma'o
nānū
naupaka kahakai
naupaka kuahiwi
nehe
nuku'i'iwi
'ōhai
'ōhi'a lehua (Flowers and *liko* will be the same as on the parent plant.)
pōhuehue
po'olā nui
'uala

'ūlei
wiliwili (Flower color will be the same as on the parent plant.)

D. Species from Cuttings for Planting Out in Shade

'ie'ie
maile
mokihana

E. Species to be Propagated by Division for Planting Out in Sun

'ahu'awa (Plant small division in pot submerged 1 inch in water.)
kauna'oa
mai'a
manono
neke (Plant runners in pot submerged 1 inch in water.)
'uki'uki

F. Species to be Propagated by Division for Planting Out in Shade

'ākōlea
kupukupu
laua'e
moa
pala'ā
palai

G. Species Not Recommended for Propagation

'Aiakanēnē, kūpaoa, na'ena'e, 'ōhelo, pā'iniu, kāmakahala, lepelepeamoa, 'ōha, and *'ōlapa.* We believe these species, derived from high elevations, will not readily adapt to lowland conditions; although some plants may survive, they will be atypical and not acceptable for use in *lei makamae.*

Pala must be propagated from spores or small

167

plants collected in the wild, which are unaccept-
able practices.

Wāwae'iole and the several kinds of *limu* are
extremely difficult to propagate. Beginners
should concentrate on plants from the lists
above.

Two recent publications offer excellent, detailed
information on general propagation of native
Hawaiian plant species. They provide highly
detailed information about the environments in
which wild populations of native species thrive.
Well illustrated and up-to-date, these books also
are informative about media mixes, plant pests,
and diseases. Heidi L. Bornhorst's *Growing
Native Hawaiian Plants* and John L. Culliney and
Bruce Koebele's *A Native Hawaiian Garden* are
inexpensive books, and both are available
through the Hawaii State Library System.

REFERENCES

1. Abbott, Isabella A. 1992. *Laʻau Hawaiʻi: Traditional Hawaiian Uses of Plants.* Honolulu: Bishop Museum Press. P. 9, *ʻauwai;* p. 47, *limu* (names by island); pp. 116 and 122, *limu kala;* p. 116, *lei limu pāhapaha* (in *hula*); p. 122, *hula* costuming; p. 123, *Makalapua* chant; p. 124, *lei palaoa;* p. 125, *kukui*-nut *lei;* p. 126, *lei poʻo kou, lei pūkiawe, lei ʻulei, lei liko lehua, lei kukui;* p. 127, *lei ʻaʻaliʻi;* p. 145 n. 33, *lauaʻe* = Microsorum spectrum.

2. Anderson-Wong, Puanani O. Unpublished ms. In: Jodi Stevens and Will McClatchey, eds., "Building Bridges with Traditional Knowledge: An Exploration of Ethnoscience in the Pacific Islands." Returning the beloved plant *lauaʻe maoli* to the Hawaiian people and clarifying the role of the invasive alien *lauaʻe* fern hold significance for cultural and natural conservation efforts.

3. Armstrong, R. Warwick. 1973. *Atlas of Hawaii.* Honolulu: University of Hawaiʻi Press.

4. Barrère, Dorothy, Mary Kawena Pukui, and Marion Kelly. 1980. *The Hula: Hawaiʻi's Own Dance.* Honolulu: Pacific Anthropological Records no. 30, Department of Anthropology, Bernice P. Bishop Museum.

5. Beckwith, Martha W. 1970. *Hawaiian Mythology.* Honolulu: University of Hawaiʻi Press. (First published in 1940 by Yale University Press.) P. 22, legend of ʻAi ʻAi and *honu;* p. 93, significance of fragrance and color; p. 93 n, *pua nukuʻiʻiwi* sacred to Laka; p. 187, legend of Kaohelo *(lei ʻōhelo);* p. 212, *kī lei;* p. 300, *kauā.*

6. Beckwith, Martha W. 1932. *Kepelino's Traditions of Hawaii.* Bernice P. Bishop Museum Bulletin no. 95. Honolulu: Bishop Museum Press. Reprint, Millwood, N.Y.: Kraus, 1978. P. 142, "The Slave Class."

7. Beckwith, Martha W. 1972. *The Kumulipo.* Chicago: University of Chicago Press, 1951; reprint, Honolulu: University Press of Hawaiʻi. P. 101, *koa.*

8. Bird, Isabela L. 1998. *Six Months in the Sandwich Islands.* London: 1873. Reprint, Honolulu: Mutual Publishing Co. P. 53, *ʻōhelo;* p. 57, *ʻukiʻuki;* p. 60, *lei ʻukiʻuki, lei ʻōhelo;* p. 159, *wāwaeʻiole;* p. 160, *lei* of "mosses" and *lei* of hibiscus.

9. Bornhorst, Heidi L. 1996. *Growing Native Hawaiian Plants.* Honolulu: The Bess Press.

10. Brigham, William T. 1911. *Ka Hana Kapa.* Vol. 3. Honolulu: Bishop Museum Press. P. 152, *ʻukiʻuki.*

11. Buck, Peter H. 1964. *Arts and Crafts of Hawaii.* Special Publication no. 45. Honolulu: Bishop Museum Press. P. 6, list of wild plants eaten by Hawaiians; colorful lobeliad flowers (*ʻōhā* and others) near habitations.

12. Ching, Patrick. 2001. *Sea Turtles of Hawaiʻi.* Honolulu: University of Hawaiʻi Press.

13. Culliney, John L., and Bruce P. Koebele. 1999. *A Native Hawaiian Garden: How to Grow and Care for Island Plants.* Honolulu: University of Hawaiʻi Press.

14. Degener, Otto. 1975. *Plants of Hawaii National Parks.* Ann Arbor, Mich.: Braun Brumfield. P. 191, *alani* fruit aromatic.

15. Desha, Stephen L. 2000. *Kamehameha and His Warrior Kekūhaupi'o*. Translated by Frances N. Frazier. Honolulu: Kamehameha Schools Press. Published with assistance from the State of Hawai'i Historic Preservation Division, Department of Land and Natural Resources. P. 156, *lei palaoa*.

16. Elbert, Samuel H., and Noelani Mahoe. 1970. *Nā Mele o Hawai'i Nei*. Honolulu: University of Hawai'i Press. P. 35, "Aloha 'Oe," *lei lehua 'āhihi*; p. 75, "Makalapua," *lei kamani, lei pua kī, lei kāmakahala*; p. 44, "He Inoa nō Ka'iulani," *laua'e*.

17. Ellis, William. 1963. *Journal of William Ellis, 1822–1823*. London: 1827. Reprint, Honolulu: Advertiser Publishing Co. (reprint of 1917 and 1928 editions). P. 44, *lei nānu*; p. 185, *kī*.

18. Emerson, Nathaniel B. 1977. *Unwritten Literature of Hawaii: The Sacred Songs of the Hula*. Washington, D.C.: Government Printing Office, 1909. Reprint, Rutland, Vt.: Charles E. Tuttle Co. P. 18, "A Prayer of Adulation to Laka"; p. 19, "Altar Prayer to Laka," and *kuahu hula*; p. 20, *kī*; pp. 21–22, *"Pule Kuahu"* (Altar Prayer); p. 42 n, *'a'ali'i* and *nuku'i'iwi*; p. 49, *"Mele Kupe'e,"* *kupukupu*; p. 56, *kuahu hula* and *lei*; p. 105 n, *lei mokihana*; p. 69, *lei ko'oko'olau*, travel wreath in "Hole Waimea"; p. 111, *lei hinahina kū kahakai*, see chant; p. 121, *lei 'ākōlea* and "Song of the Tree-Shell"; p. 209 n, *'ōhai*; p. 223, *Hula 'Īlio* and *lei hīnano*.

19. Emerson, Nathaniel B. 1978. *Pele and Hi'iaka: A Myth from Hawaii*. Honolulu: Star Bulletin Ltd., 1915. Reprint, Rutland, Vt: Charles E. Tuttle Company. Introduction, p. xxvi, *lei lehua* and *lei kauna'oa*; p. 5, *lei hala*; p. 19, *lei pala'ā*; p. 52, *uhiuhi*; p. 67 n, *lei hala*; p. 125, *lei 'ie'ie*; p. 159, *lei laua'e-o-Kalalau*; p. 162, Hi'iaka's view from Pohakea; p. 167, *lei ākulikuli 'ae'ae, lei 'ilima*, and *lei wiliwili*; p. 191, Hi'iaka and Lohi'au; p. 191, *lehua*.

20. Fornander, Abraham. 1986. *Hawaiian Antiquities and Folk Lore*. Vol. 4, pt. 2. Honolulu: Bishop Museum Press, 1917. Reprint, Millwood New York: Kraus. P. 220, *lei palaoa wiliwili*; p. 380, *naupaka*; p. 390, l. 472, *lei 'āhihi*; p. 392, ll. 538–539, *wiliwili*; p. 392, ll. 565–566, *lei kou*; p. 566, the four *maile* sisters.

21. Fornander, Abraham. 1986. *Hawaiian Antiquities and Folk Lore*. Vol. 4, pt. 3. Honolulu: Bishop Museum Press, 1917. Reprint, Millwood, N.Y.: Kraus. p. 558, legend of Puapualenalena; p. 576 n, Kapi'olani.

22. Fornander, Abraham. 1986. *Hawaiian Antiquities and Folk Lore*. Vol. 5. Honolulu: Bishop Museum Press, 1918–1919. Reprint, Millwood, N.Y.: Kraus. P. 62, *lei pāhapaha*.

23. Fornander, Abraham. 1985. *Hawaiian Antiquities and Folk Lore*. Honolulu: Bishop Museum Press, 1920. Vol. 5, pt. 3. Reprint, Millwood, N.Y.: Kraus. P. 576, "Story of Kaohelo."

24. Fornander, Abraham. 1985. *Hawaiian Antiquities and Folk Lore*. Vol. 6, pt. 3. Honolulu: Bishop Museum Press, 1920. Reprint, Millwood, N.Y.: Kraus. P. 540 n, *lei kāmakahala*.

25. Gaudichaud, Charles D. "The Vegetation of the Sandwich Islands as Seen by Charles Gaudichaud in 1819." *Le Voyage Autour du Monde*. Vol. 4, book 2. Botanique Îsles Sandwich. Paris, 1826–1830. Occasional Papers of the Bernice P. Bishop Museum, Honolulu, 1983. A Translation, with Notes,

of Gaudichaud's "Îsles Sandwich" (1826). Harold St. John and Margaret Titcomb. P. 15, Hawaiians and *lei* making; *lei hala, lei kou, lei ʻilima, lei ʻōhiʻa ʻai (hua), lei wiliwili, lei ʻāwikiwiki, lei maile, lei maiʻa.*

26. Gibson, M., ed. *Nu Hou* (The Hawaiian News). March 21, 1873. *Lei nānū.*

27. Gutmanis, June. 1983. *Nā Pule.* Honolulu: Kahiko Editions Ltd. P. 52, "Milk for the Child"; p. 101, surfing.

28. Gutmanis, June. 1976. *Kahuna Laʻau Lapaʻau.* Norfolk Island, Australia: Island Heritage Ltd. P. 23, *lei limu kala;* p. 85, *lei lāʻī;* p. 112, *lei wauke mālolo.*

29. Handy, E. S. Craighill, and Mary Kawena Pukui. 1958. *The Polynesian Family System in Kaʻū, Hawaii.* The Polynesian Society, Wellington, N.Z. Reprint, Charles E. Tuttle Company, Japan, 1972 (3rd printing, 1976). Pp. 28, 39, Hawaiian "one-ness with nature"; p. 137, *lei koʻokoʻolau;* p. 215, *ʻaʻaliʻi* and *koʻoloa ʻula;* p. 217, *kūpaoa.*

30. Handy, E. S. Craighill, E. G. Handy, and M. K. Pukui. 1972. *Native Planters in Old Hawaii.* Bernice P. Bishop Museum Bulletin no. 233. Honolulu: Bishop Museum Press. P. 11, ti-leaf *lei;* p. 25, *ʻauwai;* p. 35, *lei kī, ʻawapuhi, maiʻa;* p. 59, *ʻauwai, lei koali, lei neke, lei maiʻa;* p. 108, *kalo, lei maile, lei ʻilima;* p. 215, *ʻaʻaliʻi;* p. 222, *kī;* p. 227, *ʻilima;* p. 233, hibiscus; p. 240, *ʻuala* and *pōhuehue;* p. 236, *lei* plants—*pala* with *maile, liko, pūkiawe* fruit; p. 305, *aliʻi nui* and *lei ʻilima.*

31. Hillebrand, William. 1888. *Flora of the Hawaiian Islands.* New York: B. Westerman and Co. P. 291 n, *lei kāmakahala;* p. 543, *pala;* p. 573, *neke.*

32. Iʻi, John P. 1959. *Fragments of Hawaiian History.* Bishop Museum Press. Translated by Mary Kawena Pukui, edited by Dorothy Barrère. P. 64, *lei palapalai, maile;* p. 172, *lei palapalai.*

33. Imada, Clyde T., and L. Pyle. 1999. "Hawaiian Botanical Society Newsletter." Vol. 38 (3–4): 49. "Waiʻanae Trail Plant List," *Melicope oahuensis* and *alani* spp

34. Johnson, Rubellite K. 1981. *Kumulipo: The Hawaiian Hymn of Creation.* Honolulu: Topgallant Publishing Co. P. 126, color red associates with *hala ʻula.* R. K. Johnson, pers. comm., red *hala.*

35. Judd, Laura F. 1928. *Honolulu: Sketches of the Life, Social, Political, and Religious in the Hawaiian Islands from 1828 to 1861.* Randolph, N.Y., 1880. Reprint, *Honolulu Star Bulletin.* P. 20, *lei ʻōhai.*

36. Kalakaua, David. 1991. *The Legends and Myths of Hawaii.* New York: C. L. Webster & Co., 1888. Reprint, Rutland, Vt., and Tokyo: Charles E. Tuttle Co. P. 339, *ti* leaf; p. 451, *lei nānū.*

37. Kamakau, Samuel M. 2000. *Nā Poʻe Kahiko: The People of Old.* Translated by Mary Kawena Pukui. From the Hawaiian newspaper *Ke Au ʻOkoʻa* (The Independent Era). Honolulu: Bishop Museum Press, 1964. Reprint of 1964 edn. P. 8, *kauwā;* p. 131, *lei pāpahi, maʻo* and *ʻilima;* p. 133, *lei pāpahi.*

38. Kaopuiki, Solomon. June 3–4, 1997, interviews with Marie McDonald during a field trip on Lānaʻi (Poliahu and *honu*); April 24, 2001, field trip to Poliahu with Marie McDonald and Paul Weissich (common name "beach vitex"); October 18, 2002, pers. comm. to Marie McDonald (anthem written around 1920).

39. Kaualilinoe, J. W. K. Excerpts from *Kalelealuakā Ku Okoa,* May 21, 1870. Translated by Kepā Maly. *Maile lau li'i* and *lei niu.*

40. Kawelo, Ho'ohila, and Maiki Lake. "A Collection of Traditional Chants." Unpublished ms.

41. Keonaona, Julia, and S. Desha, Sr. Sept. 18, 1924–July 17, 1928. "He Mo'olelo Ka'ao no Hi'iaka-i-ka-poli-o Pele" (A legendary tale of Hi'iaka, who is held in the bosom of Pele). From the Hawaiian newspaper *Ka Hoku o Hawai'i* (The Star of Hawaii). Excerpts translated by Kepā Maly. Dec. 14, 1926, *lei maile lau li'i; lei lehua; lei hīnano* and *lei hala.* November 23, 1926, Hi'iaka; *lei 'ilima;* Feb. 15, 1927, *lei ma'o; 'ōhai; lei kukui; lei ma'o; lei kauna'oa.*

42. Kihe, John Whalley, and Hermosa Isaac. 1914, 1924. The Hawaiian newspaper *Ka Hoku o Hawai'i* (The Star of Hawaii). Translated by Kepā Maly. *Lei ko'oko'olau.*

43. Kihe, John W. H. I., J. Wise, et al. May 7, 1914. "Ka'ao Ho'oniua Pu'uwai No Ka-Miki," in the Hawaiian newspaper *Ka Hoku o Hawai'i* (The Star of Hawaii). Excerpts translated by Kepā Maly. *Lei maile, lei pālai, lei 'ie'ie, lei lehua, lei kupali'i, lei na'ena'e,* and *lei kūpaoa.*

44. Kirch, Patrick V. 1985. *Feathered Gods and Fishhooks.* Honolulu: University of Hawai'i Press. P. 109, Menehune Ditch, engineering skills; pp. 302–303, cultural development period; p. 197, *lei niho palaoa.*

45. Krauss, Beatrice H. 1972. *Ethnobotany of Hawaii.* Honolulu: Department of Botany, University of Hawai'i.

46. Krauss, Beatrice H. 2001. *Plants in Hawaiian Medicine.* Honolulu: University of Hawai'i Press. P. 76, *limu kala.*

47. Macrae, James. 1972. *With Lord Byron at the Sandwich Islands in 1825. Being Extracts from the MS Diary of Macrae, Scottish Botanist.* Compiled by William F. Wilson. (First published in 1922, Honolulu.) Reprint, Honolulu: Petroglyph Ltd. P. 11, *lei 'ilima* opp. p. 66, *nuku'i'iwi* sketch; p. 67, *nuku'i'iwi;* p. 192, *lama.*

48. Malo, David. 1980. *Hawaiian Antiquities* (Mo'olelo Hawaii). Translated by Nathaniel B. Emerson, 1898. Bernice P. Bishop Museum Special Publication no. 2. 2d ed. Honolulu: Bishop Museum Press. P. 128, *lei 'ie'ie;* pp. 143–144, *lei pala;* pp. 148–149, *pala* decorates the *akua poko.*

49. Maly, Kepā. 1977. April 27, 2000, pers. comm. with Marie McDonald concerning *lei 'ōlapa, lei mānewanewa,* and *"mānewanewa"* as an old Lāna'i expression.

50. McDonald, Marie A. 1998. "An Overview of Laua'e in Hawaiian Lore and Cultural Practice, with Historical Notes." Compiled by Kepā Maly. Unpublished ms. *'A'ali'i kū makani.* Kohala Mountains as source for *lei* materials (pers. comm. with Hannah Purdy Lekelesa and Mary Leialoha Ka'ilianu Bell, 1975).

51. Meyen, Franz J. F. 1981. *A Botanist's Visit to Hawaii, 1831.* Excerpts from the original publication, *Trip Around the World on the Royal Prussian Ship Princess Louise, 1830–1832.* Excerpt translated from

the original German by Astrid Jackson. Honolulu: Press Pacifica. P. ix, Gaudichaud collection of lobeliads; p. 12, *Edwardsia chrysophylla,* old name for Sophora chrysophylla *(māmane),* worn in hair *(lei po'o);* p. 42, Gaudichaud's lobeliads (*'ōhā* and others).

52. Nagata, Kenneth. *Hawaiian Journal of History* 19 (1985): 42. Table 2, pride of Barbados, 1830.

53. Neal, Marie C. 1965. *In Gardens of Hawaii.* Bernice P. Bishop Museum Special Publication no. 50. Honolulu: Bishop Museum Press. P. 714, *lei kou.*

54. Pukui, Mary Kawena, and Samuel H. Elbert. 1986. *Hawaiian Dictionary.* Honolulu: University of Hawai'i Press. P. 3, *'a'ali'i* and *a'e;* p. 29, *lei 'āpiki;* pp. 50–52, *lei hala;* p. 54, *uhiuhi;* p. 120, *kala;* p. 166, *ko'olau;* p. 185, *kūpaoa;* p. 192, *lama;* p. 201, *lei-o-Hi'iaka* and *lei pāpahi;* p. 204, *lei lepelepeamoa;* p. 207, *lei limu kala;* p. 303, *pa'iniu.*

55. Pukui, Mary Kawena, Samuel H. Elbert, and Esther Mookini. 1976. *Place Names of Hawaii.* Honolulu: University of Hawai'i Press. P. 61, "Ka'ena" and *honu;* p. 188, "Polihale" and *limu pāhapaha;* p. 188, "Polihua" and *honu.*

56. Rock, Joseph F. A. 1919. *Monographic Study of the Hawaiian Species of the Tribe Lobelioideae, Family Campanulaeae.* Honolulu: Bishop Museum Press. P. 152, *pua 'ala;* pp. 157–159, colorful lobeliads.

57. Rock, Joseph F. A. 1974. *The Indigenous Trees of the Hawaiian Islands.* Privately published, 1913. Reprint, Tokyo: Charles E. Tuttle. P. 191, *lei wiliwili;* p. 197, lemon-scented Zanthoxylom; p. 305, *Kokia drynarioides* (= Rock's *Kokia rockii*).

58. Rock, Joseph F. A. 1913. *List of Hawaiian Names of Plants.* Honolulu: Hawaiian Gazette Co.

59. Rock, Joseph F. A. 1917. *Ornamental Trees of Hawaii.* Privately published.

60. St. John, Harold. 1973. *List and Summary of the Flowering Plants in the Hawaiian Islands.* Pacific Tropical Botanical Garden Memoir no. 1. Lāwa'i, Kaua'i: Pacific Tropical Botanical Garden Press. P. 179, *'ōhai.*

61. Sinclair, Frances. 1888. *Indigenous Flowers of the Hawaiian Islands.* London: Samson Low, Marston, Searle, and Rivington. P. 6, *lei 'āwikiwiki* and *wiliwili.*

62. Stemmerman, Lani. 1981. *A Guide to Pacific Wetland Plants.* Honolulu: U.S. Army Corps of Engineers. P. 29, *neke.*

63. Sterling, Elspeth P., and Catherine C. Summers. 1978. *Sites of O'ahu.* Honolulu: Bishop Museum Press.

64. Stewart, Charles S. 1970. *Journal of a Residence in the Sandwich Islands During the Years 1823–1824–1825.* Facsimile of the 3d edn. by University of Hawai'i Press, 1830. P. 364, Hawaiians fond of purple, and purple globe amaranth grown for *lei.*

65. Taylor, William R. 1960. *Marine Algae of the Eastern Tropical and Subtropical Coasts of the Americas.* University of Michigan Studies, Scientific Series, vol. 21. Ann Arbor: University of Michigan Press.

66. Thrum, Thomas G., comp. 1912. *Hawaiian Folk Tales.* Chicago: A. C. McClurg and Co. Ch. 9, Dr. N. B. Emerson and the story of Kalelealuakā. Pt. 1, p. 74, Kalelealuakā; pt. 2, p. 82, supernatural powers; pt. 3, battles, *lei maile lau liʻi, lei ʻahuʻawa, lei hala, lei hinahina kū kahakai, lei kō.*

67. Valier, Kathy. 1995. *Ferns of Hawaii.* Honolulu: University of Hawaiʻi Press.

68. Wagner, Warren L., Derral L. Herbst, and S. H. Sohmer. 1990. *Manual of the Flowering Plants of Hawaiʻi.* Honolulu: University of Hawaiʻi Press and Bishop Museum Press. P. 155, *ʻuala* cultivars.

69. Westervelt, William D. 1991. *Hawaiian Legends of Volcanoes.* Rutland, Vt., and Tokyo: Charles E. Tuttle Co. P. 55, "Pele and the Snow Goddess."

70. Wichman, Frederick B. 1991. *Polihale and Other Kauaʻi Legends.* Honolulu: Bamboo Ridge Press.

71. Wilson, Kenneth A. "Alien Ferns in Hawaiʻi." *Pacific Science* 50 (2): 127–141 (1996), *lauaʻe.*

INDEX

Main entry pages are in **bold type.**

making, 26; chiefly house dedication, 58; early documentation, xiii; forgiveness, 74; healing, 74; image dedication, 17; *kauwā* sacrifice, 32; nursing mothers, 143; *'ōhi'a* log selection, 17; purification, 17

Cheirodendron trigynum. See *'ōlapa*

Clermontia kohalae. See *'ōhā*

clubmoss. See *wāwae'iole*

coastal sandalwood. See *'iliahialo'e*

coconut. See *niu*

Cocos nucifera. See *niu*

collecting *lei* materials: chant, 84–85; laws and regulations, 165; protocol, xiv

conservation of *lei* plants, xiv

Coprosma ernodeoides. See *'aiakanēnē*

Cordia subcordata. See *kou*

Cordyline fruticosa. See *kī*

cotton, Hawaiian. See *ma'o*

cultivated *lei* plants, 165

cultural context for *lei*, xiii–xiv

Cuscuta sandwichiana. See *kauna'oa*

cuttings, propagation by, 167

Cyclosorus interruptus. See *neke*

Dianella sandwicensis. See *'uki'uki*

division, propagation by, 167

dodder. See *kauna'oa*

Dodonaea viscosa. See *'a'ali'i*

Dubautia ciliolata subsp. *ciliolata.* See *na'ena'e*

Dubautia scabra. See *kūpaoa*

ehu. See *'ōlapa*

'ehu'awa. See *'ahu'awa*

eluehe. See *'ūlei*

Emerson, Nathaniel B., xiii, 16, 22, 30, 59, 115

Emma, Queen, 31

endangered species, 165

Erythrina sandwicensis. See *wiliwili*

fern, whisk. See *moa*

ferns. See *'ākōlea, kupukupu, laua'e neke, pala, pala'ā,* and *palai*

fishing, 134

forgiveness ceremony, 74

fragrant *lei* materials, 14, 58; flowers, 12, 22, 23–25, 28, 34, 46, 95, 96–97, 99, 124, 139; foliage, 6, 13, 57, 61, 80–85, 89, 90, 128, 131; fruit, 94

Freycinetia arborea. See *'ie'ie*

Gardenia brighamii. See *nānū*

gathering *lei* materials. See collecting *lei* materials

Gaudichaud–Beaupré, Charles, xiii, 16, 30, 44, 79, 107

Geranium cuneatum subsp. *hololeucum.* See *nohoanu*

ginger, shampoo. See *'awapuhi*

Gossypium tomentosum. See *ma'o*

gourd. See *ipu*

Hā'ena, 61

hāhā. See *'ōhā, 'ōlulu,* and *pua 'ala*

hala (Pandanus tectorius), 7, **16–19,** 31, 158, 165, 166; ceremonial significance, 17; colors, 17; *'īkoi,* 17, 19; in lei, 17, 18, 19, 40, 46, 62, 69, 86; *lihilihi 'ula,* 17, 19; *melemele,* 17, 19; *pia,* 17; *'ula,* 17, 19. See also *hīnano*

hala pepe (Pleomele hawaiiensis), **20,** 80, 158, 165, 166; in *lei,* 20

hanupaoa. See *kūpaoa* and *na'ena'e*

hau (Hibiscus tiliaceus), **21,** 158, 165, 166, 167; in *lei,* 21

hau hele 'ula. See *koki'o*

hau ka'eka'e. See *hau*

hau ko'i'i. See *hau*

hau oheohe. See *hau*

Hawaiian cotton. See *ma'o*

kamani *(Calophyllum inophyllum)*, **34–35,** 159, 165, 166; in *lei,* 34, 35

kamanu. See *kamani*

Kamehameha I, 96

Kamehameha III (King Kauikeaouli), 108

Ka–Miki, 58

Kanahele, Pualani Kanaka'ole, xv, 34

Kanaloa, 14, 77, 79, 89

Kane, 25, 77, 128

kānehoa. See *pūkiawe*

Ka'ōhelo, 111

Kapi'olani, Chiefess, 111

Kapo, 16, 104

kapua'ilio. See *pala*

kauhi. See *'ākia*

Kauikeaouli, King (Kamehameha III), 108

kauila māhu. See *'ōlapa*

kauna'oa (Cuscuta sandwichiana), 11, **36–37,** 159, 167; in *lei,* 11, 36, 37

kauna'oa kahakai. See *kauna'oa*

kauna'oa lei. See *kauna'oa*

kauno'a. See *kauna'oa*

Kaunolū, 96

kauwā, 32

kāwa'u. See *a'e (Zanthoxylum dipetalum)* and *uhiuhi*

kawau kua kuku kapa. See *a'e (Zanthoxylum dipetalum)*

kea. See *uhiuhi*

Keawa'ula, 31

Keōpūolani, Queen, 96

kī (Cordyline fruticosa), 14, **38–39,** 159, 165, 167; *lā'ī* defined, 39; in *lei,* 14, 37, 38

Kiha, 111

kino lau, xiv; defined, xiii; of Kanaloa, 77, 89

Kīpuka–kai–o–Kīlauea, 31

kō (Saccharum officinarum), 7, **40–41,** 159, 165, 167; in *lei,* 40, 41

koa (Acacia koa), **42,** 159, 166; in *lei,* 42. See also *koai'a*

koai'a (Acacia koaia or *A. koa),* **43,** 159, 166; in *lei,* 43. See also *koa*

koai'e. See *koai'a*

koali (Ipomoea carica), **44,** 159, 167; in *lei,* 44

koali 'ai. See *koali*

koali 'ai'ai. See *koali*

koali lau manamana. See *koali*

koa 'ohā. See *koai'a*

Kokia drynarioides. See *koki'o*

koki'o (Kokia drynarioides), **45,** 159, 165, 166; in *lei,* 45. See also *koki'o 'ula*

koki'o kea. See *koki'o ke'oke'o*

koki'o ke'oke'o (Hibiscus arnottianus subsp. *punaluuensis),* **46,** 159, 165, 166, 167; in *lei,* 46

koki'o 'ula (Hibiscus kokia), **47,** 159, 165, 166, 167; in *lei,* 47

koki'o 'ula'ula. See *koki'o 'ula*

kokolau. See *ko'oko'olau*

kōko'olau. See *ko'oko'olau*

kōlea. See *kōlea lau li'i*

kōlea lau li'i (Myrsine sandwicensis), **48,** 160, 167; in *lei,* 66, 67

kolikukui. See *'ilima*

kolokolo kahakai (Vitex rotundifolia), **48–49,** 160, 166, 167; in *lei,* 49. See also *mānewanewa*

Kona agricultural system, 45

ko'okolau. See *ko'oko'olau*

ko'oko'olau (Bidens menziesii subsp. *filiformis),* **50–51,** 145, 160, 166, 167; in *lei,* 51. See also *po'olā nui*

ko'olau. See *ko'oko'olau*

ko'oloa'ula (Abutilon menziesii), **52,** 160, 165, 166, 167; in *lei,* 52

kou (Cordia subcordata), **53–54,** 160, 165, 166; in *lei,* 53, 54

Ku, 26, 77, 143

kuahu hula, 10, 14, 20, 26, 42, 55, 59, 61, 80, 120, 131. See also *hula* and Laka

Kuali'i, 99

MARIE McDONALD, ethnologist, educator, and master *lei* maker, was recognized as a "Master of Traditional Arts" by the National Endowment for the Arts in 1990. Her first book, *Ka Lei*, remains in print after a quarter century. She credits her Hawaiian mother for her early awareness of the importance of *lei* in traditional family and community life.

PAUL WEISSICH directed the Honolulu Botanical Gardens system for more than three decades. He received the Medal of Merit (1988) and the Distinguished Service Medal (1991) from the Garden Club of America. He is a consultant and landscape architect and is coauthor of *Plants for Tropical Landscapes: A Gardener's Guide.*